Distant Thunder

Distant Thunder

An Integrated
Skills Approach to
Learning Language
through Literature

Janis G. Scalone

PITT Pitt Series in English as a Second Language

Ann Arbor
THE UNIVERSITY OF MICHIGAN PRESS

Illustrated by Jacob Kindlesparker

Mom, you taught me that even the most difficult times are surmountable. From you, Dad, I learned that the best reward for a job well done is simply knowing that it is so. Thank you both for all the lessons you have taught me. And Pooky, thanks for always being there—no matter what.

Preface

Whenever I think of the words *distant thunder,* I imagine a hot summer's day coming to a close, storm clouds on the horizon, the faintest rumble of thunder. The title of this book emerged slowly from this persistent image–one I couldn't, and in truth didn't, want to shake. As I went about the long task of finding, reading, and selecting literature for the book, this image kept coming to mind. It seemed somehow appropriate. Since multicultural literature in general is only gradually being added to the traditional literary canon, for me, the voices of the characters in this text (and of the authors themselves) resembled thunder just beyond the horizon. Like the distant thunder, their voices might be only faintly heard by the mainstream, but like thunder, they presage a swell of power, energy, even fury coming its way. Although the voices remain for now on the periphery, as you will discover, they are nonetheless powerful for the reader who "hears" their rumblings.

Acknowledgments

Grateful acknowledgment is made to the following authors, publishers, and agents for permission to reprint previously published material.

Francisco Jiménez for "The Circuit." Used by permission of the author. The story also appears in *The Circuit: Stories from the Life of a Migrant Child* by Francisco Jiménez, University of New Mexico Press.

Chitra Divakaruni for "Doors." Used by permission of the author.

New York Quarterly for "Farewell" by Liz Sohappy Bahe.

Leona P. Schecter, Literary Agent, for "Jobs" by Wendy Wilder Larsen and Tran Thi Nga.

José Antonio Burciaga for "La Puerta." Used by permission of the author.

Nicolas C. Vaca for "The Purchase." First appeared in *El Espejo,* copyright 1969. Used by permission of the author.

Mykel D. Myles for "Saturday Morning Memorial." First appeared in *Saturday Morning Memorial.* Used by permission of the author.

International Publishing Company and Ahsahta Press for "Thomas Iron-Eyes" by Marnie Walsh. The poem also appears in Walsh's *A Taste of the Knife,* copyright 1976, fourth printing 1994, Ahsahta Press at Boise State University.

The Christian Science Publishing Society for "Unfolding Bud" by Naoshi Koriyama.

Hisaye Yamamoto and Kitchen Table: Women of Color Press for "Wilshire Bus." Originally published in *Pacific Citizen,* Dec. 23, 1950. From *Seventeen Syllables and Other Stories,* Kitchen Table: Women of Color Press, 1988. Used by permission of the author and of Kitchen Table: Women of Color Press, P.O. Box 988, Latham, New York 12110.

Every effort has been made to trace the ownership of all copyrighted materials in this book and to obtain permission for their use.

I also wish to thank the following individuals who helped make the book a reality. Dr. Lionel Menasche, Department of Linguistics, University of Pittsburgh, my mentor, former professor, and best critic, for his invaluable advice and patient encouragement throughout the project. I thank him especially for seeing potential in the graduate school project I submitted in the summer of 1992, a project that later became the seed for this book. Kelly Sippell, University of Michigan Press acquisitions editor, who, after a year's worth of e-mail messages, feels like a friend. I thank her for calmly answering my many frantic inquiries and gently nudging me toward the finish line. Dr. Linda Lonon Blanton, Department of English, University of New Orleans, and Dr. Gayle Nelson, Department of Applied Linguistics/ESL, Georgia State University, for their reviews and invaluable suggestions for improvement. Colleagues Norman Prange and Luis Perez for double-checking my English translations of Spanish words. Former Liberal Arts Dean Dr. Ron Key of Cuyahoga Community College for helping me keep the book "on the front burner." Cuyahoga Community College reference librarians Dr. Shahrokh Afshar, Pat Gabriel, and Brent Kabasta for their help in locating materials and hard-to-find authors. Colleague Dr. John Eble for his support and friendship. Colleague Dr. Kay Rice for her words of encouragement and her prayers. My neighbors Jake and Susan Kindlesparker for their emotional support and for being the best of neighbors always. Carol Jasnow and Kim Pradhan, ESL teachers at the University of Pittsburgh's English Language Institute, for classroom testing several units and providing me with helpful feedback. The following Cuyahoga Community College students for their comments, suggestions, and contagious enthusiasm during the spring of 1997, all of which helped me better see the book through students' eyes: Durgesh Agarwal, Wei-hu Cheng, Insun Choi, Viktoriya Dymova, Caesar Augusto Mugaburu Garcia, Giselle E. Mugaburu Garcia, Agueda Pulpillo Herrera, Seung (Sean) Hong, Zorya Novik, Edmira Shipcka, Nadezhda Tashayeva, José Emilio de Ramón Vilar, and Xhing min Zhang. Each of these individuals contributed in his or her own way to the completion of this book. However, any shortcomings contained within are mine alone.

Contents

To the Teacher   xv
Introduction   1

Unit 1.   "Doors," a Short Story by Chitra Divakaruni   4
Meet the Author
Preparing to Read
The First Reading
A Closer Look
Sharing the Possibilities
Understanding Character
Extending the Reading Experience
Focus on Language

Unit 2.   "Farewell," a Poem by Liz Sohappy Bahe   18
Meet the Author
Preparing to Read
The First Reading
A Closer Look
Sharing the Possibilities
Understanding What a Poem Does
Extending the Reading Experience
Focus on Language

Unit 3.   "La Puerta," a Short Story by José Antonio Burciaga   25
Meet the Author
Preparing to Read
The First Reading
A Closer Look
Sharing the Possibilities
Understanding Characterization
Extending the Reading Experience
Focus on Language

Unit 4.   "Jobs," a Poem by Wendy Wilder Larsen and Tran Thi Nga   41
Meet the Authors
Preparing to Read
The First Reading
A Closer Look

Sharing the Possibilities
Understanding Poetic Meaning
Extending the Reading Experience
Focus on Language

Unit 5.   "The Circuit," a Short Story by Francisco Jiménez   47
Meet the Author
Preparing to Read
The First Reading
A Closer Look
Sharing the Possibilities
Understanding Point of View
Extending the Reading Experience
Focus on Language

Unit 6.   "The Purchase," a Short Story by Nick C. Vaca   62
Meet the Author
Preparing to Read
The First Reading
A Closer Look
Sharing the Possibilities
Understanding Setting and Mood
Extending the Reading Experience
Focus on Language

Unit 7.   "Wilshire Bus," a Short Story by Hisaye Yamamoto   77
Meet the Author
Preparing to Read
The First Reading
A Closer Look
Sharing the Possibilities
Understanding Flashbacks
Extending the Reading Experience
Focus on Language

Unit 8.   "Saturday Morning Memorial," a Poem by Mykel D. Myles   90
Meet the Author
Preparing to Read
The First Reading
A Closer Look
Sharing the Possibilities
Understanding Imagery
Extending the Reading Experience
Focus on Language

Unit 9.   **"Thomas Iron-Eyes," a Poem by Marnie Walsh**   **103**
            Meet the Author
            Preparing to Read
            The First Reading
            A Closer Look
            Sharing the Possibilities
            Understanding Simile
            Extending the Reading Experience
            Focus on Language

Notes for Teachers   **121**
Glossary of Terms   **131**
Bibliography   **133**
Additional Works of Interest   **135**

To the Teacher

Designed for adult high-intermediate to advanced ESL students, *Distant Thunder: An Integrated Skills Approach to Learning Language through Literature* contains nine units, each centering on a single short story or poem accompanied by student-centered, reader-response activities and language exercises. To reflect a *process approach* to reading literature, each unit is broken into several components.

> *Meet the Author* opens each unit with a biographical sketch of the author. Each author can be seen as a role model by ESL students (especially those newly arrived to the United States) and as testimony that success is indeed possible, even within a predominantly English-speaking environment.
>
> *Preparing to Read* provides cultural, historical, and demographic information followed by questions that ask students to draw on their own experiences for answers.
>
> *The First Reading* focuses students' attention on a purpose for reading and is the first step in getting students personally involved with the literary work.
>
> *A Closer Look* helps students relate the work to themselves as individuals, that is, to their own ideas, feelings, opinions, and perceptions of the world.
>
> *Sharing the Possibilities* encourages extended social interaction within the classroom. Such sharing of ideas helps students see that more than one interpretation of a given work is possible.
>
> *Understanding [various literary structures]* (e.g., point of view, character, setting, etc.) helps students gain a better understanding and appreciation for the craft of writing and the power of language—how words help shape the reader's response to literature.
>
> *Extending the Reading Experience* contains activities and projects that encourage students to respond *creatively* to the reading experience, to see how their imaginations can shape their individual and even collective reading experiences in very different ways. Students at times are called upon to rework endings, interview characters, even create visual and aural interpretations of the work.
>
> *Focus on Language,* the final group of activities found in each unit, is more form focused than the others as it looks at how specific language

features work. These activities are designed to help the students better understand the literary work.

Notes for Teachers contains additional background information, extra activities, suggestions for teaching, and answer keys to selected exercises. Teachers may wish to assign the additional background information as further reading for students. Answer keys are provided for closed-ended questions (one answer possible). The book contains many open-ended questions for which various answers are possible. In no way should the teacher or student feel obligated to provide just one correct answer for open-ended questions. More about this later.

The *Glossary of Terms* lists the definitions of important terms used throughout the text.

The *Bibliography* lists the resources used in the writing of this book.

The *Additional Works of Interest* section provides a list of resource books, videos, and sound recordings for those seeking more information about the various cultural groups represented in *Distant Thunder*. This section also includes a list of ancillary readings such as biographies and fiction, poetry, and drama that have themes similar to those found throughout *Distant Thunder*. Teachers are encouraged to consult the "Additional Works of Interest" section in advance for audiovisual and printed materials to use in the classroom. For example, after completing Unit 3, students might read John Steinbeck's *The Pearl* and then compare the novel's characters and their motives with those in Burciaga's "La Puerta." The videos, sound recordings, and supplementary readings listed in the "Additional Works of Interest" section will spark further discussion and lead to a deeper understanding of the issues raised by the stories and poems.

More Suggestions for Use

Distant Thunder contains authentic, high-interest short stories and poems by ethnic minority writers. Chosen for their rich themes and high readability, these stories and poems are sure to appeal to readers. The book begins with literary works that are thematically and linguistically less difficult. Since the stories and poems become progressively more difficult, the teacher may want to use the book in the order presented. (On the other hand, advanced level students may feel quite comfortable moving around the text as their interests dictate.) No matter what order is used, the teacher will find that student-centered activities are plentiful and will engage the student with the text. Teachers should feel free to adapt these activities to their individual classroom needs. Space is provided throughout the book for shorter answers to questions. At the same time, lengthy answers can be written on loose-leaf paper or in journals. Many of the activity questions lend themselves to either written or spoken responses. Students could form small discussion groups to address the questions or write their responses down. The teacher need only decide which skill requires more practice at the time. It is also important to note that teachers do not need training in the study of literature to use this book. In fact, *Distant Thunder* encourages teachers and students to explore meaning *together* and to accept any reasonable interpretation of the stories and poems. Teachers should not see themselves as "answer givers" but as *participants* in the search for meaning. What's more, *Distant Thunder* invites readers (students and teachers alike) to have fun in this pursuit.

Introduction

At one time the study of literature was considered an integral part of any second or foreign language learning experience. Literary study was believed to facilitate the language learning process. In fact, any language program without literature study was thought to be lacking in both substance and purpose. In the early 1970s, however, attitudes toward using literature in the language classroom changed. Many language teachers abandoned literature altogether, denouncing it as inappropriate, even detrimental for the English as a second or foreign language (ESL/EFL) learner.

Fortunately, there has been renewed interest in using literary works in the ESL classroom. Today's methods for using literature in the language classroom are based on sound language learning theories. In the spirit of communicative language teaching, for example, proponents of using literature suggest that a literary work can be a catalyst for meaningful and spontaneous communication. Furthermore, a number of linguists have made a strong case for including literature in a language program on the grounds that by reading literature, a nonnative speaker (NNS) can increase his or her understanding of, even tolerance for, other cultures. Literature contextualizes patterns of social interaction in ways that synthetic functional/notional dialogues cannot. Furthermore, literature reveals the codes, assumptions, and mores that color these interactions (Collie and Slater 1987).

Today's approach to using literature in the language classroom runs counter to traditional views on reading, which hold that reading is primarily a *receptive* skill. According to this notion, readers passively receive information from a printed text—the implication here is that meaning resides solely in the words themselves. As literacy expert Mike Rose says, "the encounter of the student and the text is often portrayed . . . as a *transmission*. Information, wisdom, virtue will pass from the book to the student [emphasis added]" (Zamel 1993). In this paradigm the reader emerges from the reading experience essentially unchanged, except to have gathered a few ideas from the page.

Fortunately, this traditional view of the reader has largely been abandoned. Readers are no longer seen as mere gatherers of knowledge but as active participants in constructing meaning. According to Louise Rosenblatt (1983) (among many others), a reader creates meaning via his or her *transaction* with the text. Text and reader act upon one another. "He [the author]

leads us to perceive selected images, personalities, and events in special rela-
tion to one another" (34). And yet the "reader brings to the work personality
traits, memories of past events, present needs and preoccupations, a particular mood of the moment, and a physical condition . . . elements in a never-to-
be-duplicated combination [that] determines his response to the particular
contribution of the text" (31).

Longtime advocates of using literature in the ESL/EFL classroom,
Carter and Long (1991) suggest that language teachers should focus on
knowledge *of* literature rather than on knowledge *about* literature.

> The teacher who wishes to impart knowledge *of* literature aims to
> impart personal pleasure in reading literary texts. . . . This kind of knowl-
> edge is not normally conveyed by survey lecture courses about literature;
> it is more likely to be conveyed by *activity-based, student-centered
> approaches which aim to lead to a high level of personal response and
> involvement* [emphasis added] (4).

Carter and Long (1991) also advise language teachers to connect the
NNS's life experiences to the text.

> Students will be better motivated to read a literary text if they can
> relate it to their own experience. In the first instance this means that they
> should be able to relate it to themselves as *individuals,* that is, to their own
> ideas, feelings, opinions and perceptions; then they should be able to
> relate it to their own experience of the world and, in particular, of the
> society in which they live (19).

Thus a new model for reading literature has emerged and alongside it a
new model for teaching.

> Language-based approaches are normally less concerned with the liter-
> ary text as a product and are more concerned with *processes of reading*
> [emphasis added]. A process-centered, language-based pedagogy means
> that the teacher has to come "down from the pedestal." The teacher
> becomes an *enabler,* working with students and creatively intervening to
> ensure a relevant and meaningful experience through a direct contact
> with the text (7).

If reading literature is to be a meaningful language learning experience,
teachers should assume the role of *monitor.* They should first choose texts
whose topics arouse the students' interest. They should also use activities that
encourage students to interact personally with the text so that it comes alive

for them and should also "intervene relevantly and creatively in order to augment the students' experience and to help them respond appropriately to a text" (Carter and Long 1991, 28).

The study of literature must also be a social experience; students should be given numerous opportunities to share their written and spoken responses with the teacher and with each other. In this way, students practice all four language skills.

Distant Thunder: An Integrated Skills Approach to Learning Language through Literature employs this new model of teaching by using student-centered activities and a reading-process approach. In the spirit of communicative language learning, *Distant Thunder* provides abundant opportunities for students to share their written and spoken responses. As such, all four language skills are integrated within the study of literature.

Distant Thunder encourages students and teachers to discover meaning together. It frees the teacher to act as an enabler as opposed to the *giver of answers* or the *interpreter.* Teachers can guide the students' transaction with the stories and poems using the text's many activities, ensuring a relevant and meaningful language experience with high-interest literature.

UNIT 1

"Doors" by Chitra Divakaruni

Meet the Author

Born in India, Chitra Divakaruni holds a Ph.D. in English from the University of California at Berkeley and teaches at Foothill College in the San Francisco Bay area, where she lives with her husband and two children. She has won numerous awards for her writing. Her writing covers a wide variety of subjects, but much of it is about India, especially Indian women. Her books include *Black Candle* (poetry), *Arranged Marriages* (stories), and *The Mistress of Spices* (a novel). She is currently president of Maitri, a helpline for South Asian women.

Preparing to Read

Behind Closed Doors

Many people value privacy. They enjoy, even need, seclusion. They protect their privacy with physical and mental barriers. Other people believe that privacy is not so important. They believe that physical barriers such as doors and walls actually alienate people from friends and family.

1. How important is privacy to you? On the line below, write your initials to show your personal attitude toward privacy. The extreme right means privacy has little or no importance to you. The extreme left means privacy is very important to you. In between these two extremes lies a range of attitudes about privacy.

Privacy is very important.   Privacy is *not* important.

2. Share your "privacy" line with a group of your classmates. Does culture seem to influence attitude toward privacy? What about gender? What other things might influence a person's attitude toward privacy?

3. What problems can arise when two people have different views on privacy?

The First Reading

"Doors" is divided into five sections. After you finish reading a section, stop and write about it as directed on a separate sheet of paper. Then move on to the next part. Continue to read and write about each part until you finish the story. This allows you to explore your reactions as the story unfolds before your eyes.

Respond freely to what you read. Describe your feelings, ideas, opinions, or reactions. For instance, what do you think of the characters? What does the story mean to you? What do you think will happen next? and so on. As you read for the first time, resist the urge to use the dictionary.

Doors

I

It all started when Raj came to live with them.

Not that there hadn't been signs earlier. Asha's mother, for one, had warned of it right at the time of the wedding.

"It'll never work, I tell you. Here you are, living in the U.S. since you were twelve. And Deepak—he's straight out of India. Just because you took a few classes together at the University, and you liked how he talks, doesn't mean that you can live with him. What do you really know about how Indian men think? About what they expect from their women?"

"Now, Ma, don't start on that again. He's not like the others, " Asha had protested. "And besides, I can adjust, too."

On the whole Asha had been right. She and Deepak had lived together happily enough for the last three years. In all matters, as their friends often commented envyingly, they were a well-adjusted couple. In all, that is, except the matter of doors.

Deepak liked to leave them open, and Asha liked them closed.

Deepak had laughed about it at first, early in the marriage.

"Are the pots and pans from the kitchen going to come and watch us making love?" he would joke when she meticulously locked the bedroom door at night, although there were just the two of them in the house. Or, "Do you think I'm going to come in and attack you?" when she locked the bathroom door behind her with an audible click. He himself always bathed with the door open, song and steam pouring out of the bathroom with equal abandon.

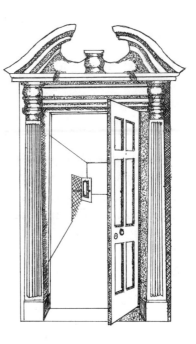

But soon he realized that it was not a laughing matter with her. Asha would shut the study door before settling down with her dissertation. When in the garden, she would make sure the gate was securely fastened as she weeded. If there had been a door to the kitchen, she would have closed it as she cooked.

Deepak was puzzled by all this door-shutting. He himself had grown up in a large family, and although they had been affluent enough to possess three bedrooms—one for Father, one for Mother and his two sisters, and the third for the three boys—they had never observed boundaries. They had constantly spilled into each others' rooms, doors always left open for the chance remark or joke.

He asked Asha about it one day. She wasn't able to give him an answer.

"I don't know. It's not like I'm shutting you out or anything. I've just always done it that way. I know it's not what you're used to. Does it bother you?"

She seemed so troubled by it that Deepak, feeling a pang of guilt, emphatically denied any feelings of unease. And really, he didn't mind. People were different. And he was more than ready to accept the unique needs of this exotic creature—Indian and yet not Indian—who had by some mysterious chance become his wife.

So things went smoothly—until Raj descended on them.

Stop! Write your response to Part I now.

II

"Tomorrow!" Asha was distraught, although she tried   15
to hide it in the face of Deepak's obvious delight. Her mind
raced over lists of things to be done—the guest bedroom
dusted, the sheets washed, a special welcome dinner
cooked (that entailed a trip to the grocery), perhaps some
flowers. . . . And her adviser was pressuring her for the
second chapter of the dissertation, which wasn't going
well.

"Yes, tomorrow! His plane comes in at ten-thirty at
night." Deepak waved the aerogram excitedly. "Imagine,
it's been five years since I've seen him! We used to be
inseparable back home, although he was so much
younger. He was always in and out of our house, laughing
and joking and playing pranks. I know you'll just love
him—everyone does! And see, he calls you bhaviji—sister-
in-law—already!"

At the airport, Raj was a lanky whirlwind, rushing
from the gate to throw his arms around Deepak, kissing
him soundly on both cheeks, oblivious to American stares.
Asha found his strong Bombay accent hard to follow as he
breathlessly regaled them with the news of India that had
Deepak throwing back his head in loud laughter.

But the trouble really started after dinner.

"What a marvelous meal, Bhaviji! I can see why
Deepak is getting a pot-belly!" Raj belched in appreciation
as he pushed back his chair. "I know I'll sleep soundly
tonight—my eyes are closing already. If you tell me where
the bedclothes are, I'll bring them over and start making
my bed while you're clearing the table."

"Thanks, Raj, but I made the bed already, upstairs in   20
the guest room."

"The guest room? I'm not a guest, Bhavi! I'm going to
be with you for quite a while. You'd better save the guest
bedroom for real guests. About six square feet of space—
right here between the dining table and the sofa—is all I
need. See, I'll just move the chairs a bit."

Seeing the look on Asha's face, Deepak tried to intervene.

"Come on Raj—why not use the guest bed for tonight
since it's made already? We can work out the long-term
arrangements later."

"Aare, yaar, you know I don't like all this formal treatment. Don't you remember what fun it was to spread a big
sheet on the floor of the living room and spend the night,
all us boys together, telling stories? Have you become
Americanized, or what? Come along and help me carry the
bedclothes down. . . ."

Asha stood frozen as his sing-song voice faded beyond   25
the bend of the stairs; then she made her own way
upstairs silently. When Deepak came to bed an hour later,
she was waiting for him.

"What! Not asleep yet? Don't you have an early class to
teach tomorrow?"

"You have to leave for work early, too."

"Well, as a matter of fact I was thinking of taking a day
off tomorrow. You know—take Raj to San Francisco,
maybe."

Asha tried to subdue the jealousy she felt.

"I really don't think you should be neglecting your   30
work—but that's your own business." She tried to shake
off the displeasure that colored her voice and speak rea-
sonably. "What I do need to straighten out is this matter of
sleeping downstairs. I need to use the dining area in the
morning and I can't do it with him sleeping there." She
shuddered silently as she pictured herself trying to enjoy
her quiet morning tea with him sprawled on the floor
nearby. "By the way, just what did he mean he's going to
be here for a long time?"

"Well, he wants to stay here until he completes his
Master's—maybe a year and a half—and I told him that
was fine with us."

"You what? Isn't this my house, too? Don't I get a say
in who stays here?"

"Fine, then. Go ahead and tell him that you don't want
him to stay here. Go ahead, wake him up and tell him
tonight." There was an edge to Deepak's voice that she
hadn't heard before, and she suddenly realized, frightened, that they were having their first serious quarrel. Her
mother's face, triumphant, rose in her mind.

"You know that's not what I want. I realize how much
it means to you to have your friend here, and I'll do my
best to make him welcome. I'm just not used to having a
long-term houseguest around, and it makes things harder

when he insists on sleeping on the living room floor." Asha offered her most charming smile to her husband, desperately willing the stranger in his eyes—cold, defensive—to disappear.

It worked. He smiled back and pulled her to him, her own dear Deepak again, promising to get Raj to use the guest room, kissing the back of her neck in that delicious way that always sent shivers up her spine. As she snuggled against him with a deep sigh of pleasure, curving her body spoonlike to fit his warm hardness, Asha promised herself to do her best to accept Raj.

Stop! Write your response to Part II now.

III

It was harder than she had expected.

For the concept of doors did not exist in Raj's universe, and he ignored their physical reality—so solid and reassuring to Asha—whenever he could. He would burst into her closed study to tell her of the latest news at school, leaving the door ajar when he left. He would throw open the door to the garage, where she did the laundry, to offer help, usually just as she was folding her underwear. Even when she retreated to her little garden in search of privacy there was no escape. From the porch, he would solicitously give her advice on the drooping fuchsias, while behind him the swinging door afforded free entry to hordes of insects. Perhaps to set her an example, he left his own bedroom door wide open, so that the honest rumble of his snores assaulted Asha on her way to the bathroom every morning.

A couple of times she tried to explain to Deepak how she felt, but he responded with surprising testiness.

"What d'you mean he's driving you crazy? He's only trying to be friendly, poor chap. I should think you'd be able to open up a bit more to him. After all, we're the only family he has in this strange country."

What use was it to tell him that her own family had never intruded upon her like this? Instead, Asha took to locking herself up in the bedroom with her work in the evenings, while downstairs Deepak and Raj talked over the

35

40

old days. Often, she fell asleep over her books and woke to the sound of Deepak's irritated knocks on the door.

"I just don't understand you nowadays!" he would exclaim with annoyance. "Why must you lock the bedroom door when you're reading? Isn't that being a bit paranoid? Maybe you should talk to someone about it."

Asha would turn away in silence, thinking, it can't be forever, he can't stay with us forever, I can put up with it until he leaves, and then everything will be as before.

And so things might have continued, had it not been for one fateful afternoon.

Stop! Write your response to Part III now.

IV

It was the end of the semester, and Asha was lying on her bed, eyes closed. That morning her advisor had told her that her dissertation lacked originality and depth, and had suggested that she restructure the argument. His final comment kept resounding in her brain: "I don't know what's been wrong with you for the past few months— you've consistently produced second rate work; even your students have been complaining about you. Maybe you need a break—a semester away from school."

"Not from school—it's a semester away from home that   45
I need," she whispered now as the door banged downstairs and Raj's eager voice floated up to her.

"Bhavi, Bhavi, where are you? Have I got great news for you!"

Asha put her pillow over her head, willing him away like the dull, throbbing headaches that came to her so often nowadays. But he was at the bedroom door, knocking.

"Open up, Bhavi! I have something to show you—I aced the Math final—I was the only one who did."

"Not now, Raj, please, I'm very tired."

"What's wrong? Do you have a headache? Wait a   50
minute, I'll bring you some of my tigerbalm—excellent for headaches."

She heard his footsteps recede, then return.

"Thanks, Raj," she called out to forestall any more conversation. "Just leave it outside. I don't feel like getting up for it right now."

"Oh, you don't have to get up." And before she could refuse, Raj had opened the door—how could she have forgotten to lock it?—and had walked in.

Shocked, speechless, Asha watched Raj. He seemed to advance in slow motion across the suddenly enormous expanse of bedroom, holding a squat green bottle in his extended hand. His lips moved, but she could not hear him above the pounding in her skull. He had invaded her last sanctuary, her bedroom. He had violated her.

Through the red haze a piercing voice rose, screaming   55
at him to get out, get out right now. A hand snatched the bottle and hurled it against the wall where it shattered and fell in emerald fragments. Dimly she recognized the voice, the hand. They were hers. And then she was alone in the sudden silence.

Stop! Write your response to Part IV now.

V

The bedroom was as neat and tranquil as ever when Deepak walked in; only a very keen eye would have noted the pale stain against the far wall.

"Are you O.K.? Raj mentioned something about you not being well." And then, as his glance fell on the packed suitcase, "What's going on?"

Very calm, she told him she was leaving. She felt a mild surprise when he swore softly and violently.

"You can't leave. You're my wife. This is your house. You belong here."

She looked at him a long moment, eyes expressionless.   60

"It's Raj, isn't it? You just can't stand him, can you? Well, I guess I'll have to do something about the poor chap."

She listened silently to his footsteps fading down the stairs, listened to the long low murmur of voices from the living room, listened to the sounds of packing from the guest room. She listened as Raj said his good-byes, listened as the front door banged behind the men.

Much later she listened as Deepak told her that Raj would be staying in a hotel till he found a room on cam-

pus, listened as he stated that he would sleep in the guest room tonight, listened to his awkward bedmaking efforts. She listened as a part of herself cried out to her to go to him, apologize and offer to have Raj back, to fashion her curves to his warm hardness, to let his lips soothe her into sleep.

Then for the first time she lay down alone in the big bed and let the night cover her slowly, layer by cold layer. And when the door finally clicked shut, she did not know whether it was in the guest room or deep inside her being.

Stop! Write your response to Part V now.

A Closer Look

Reread "Doors." Then write your answers to the following questions below.

1. What do you think is the main conflict in the story?

   _____

2. Did your feelings about any of the characters *change* during subsequent readings?

   _____

3. Have you ever known anyone for whom "the concept of doors did not exist"? How did you feel about this person?

   _____

4. How do you think your *gender* and *culture* influenced your reactions to the story? What other things influenced your reactions?

   _____

Explain your answers to a classmate.

Sharing the Possibilities

Culture and gender influence how people communicate with each other. Differences in culture and gender can even cause serious misunderstandings. Answer the following questions. Then share your responses with your classmates.

1. In Part I of the story, Asha's mother says to her, "Deepak—he's straight out of India. . . . What do you really know about how Indian men think? About what they expect from their women?" Asha's mother seems to have some firsthand knowledge about how Indian men think and what they expect from women. What do you think she wants Asha to "really know"?

_____

_____

2. In Part II of the story, Raj asks Deepak if he's become "Americanized." What does Deepak do or say that causes Raj to say this?

_____

3. Even though Asha and Deepak are both natives of India, they have very different attitudes toward privacy. Why do you think this is so? Do you think gender contributes anything to the misunderstanding between Asha and Deepak? Explain.

_____

_____

4. In Part II , Asha says, "Isn't this my house, too? Don't I get a say in who stays here?" How would you answer her questions?

_____

_____

5. Reread the final paragraph of the story. What do you think is happening here? What is your interpretation of the last sentence?

_____

_____

Compare your interpretation of the last sentence with your classmates' interpretations.

Understanding Character

When authors place imaginary people into a story, they have created characters. By describing how these characters look, sound, feel, behave, and respond to each other, authors are able to make their characters seem alive.

A character's thoughts and actions can help you understand the story, so it's important for you to spend some time thinking about the characters. How do you feel about them? If you see yourself in a character, you are said to identify with him or her. For example, do you understand the frustration that Deepak feels toward Asha and her habit of closing doors? Or do you more readily see yourself in Asha and her search for solitude? And what about Raj? Do you understand his need for friendship?

1. Which character do you most identify with?

   _____

2. Give reasons why you feel close to this character.

   _____

3. Which character do you least identify with?

   _____

4. Give reasons why you don't feel close to this character.

   _____

Compare your answers to a classmate's answers.

Extending the Reading Experience

Choose one of the following activities.

A. Mind Reading

> Very calm, [Asha] told [Deepak] she was leaving. She felt a mild surprise when he swore softly and violently.
> "You can't leave. You're my wife. This is your house. You belong here."
> She looked at him a long moment, eyes expressionless.

Imagine for a moment that you are Asha. Write a paragraph in which you describe what you are thinking as you stare silently at Deepak.

B. Off Stage

Asha does not hear what Raj and Deepak say to one another right before Raj departs for a hotel. She hears only "the long low murmur of voices from the living room." What do you imagine Deepak and Raj say? Do they look at each other? Re-create the conversation you think occurs between Deepak and Raj at that fateful moment. Practice the dialogue with a classmate so that you can present it to the class.

C. Another View

Imagine that you are Raj sitting alone in your hotel room. Twenty-four hours have passed since you so hastily moved out of your friend's house. Your thoughts turn to Asha. Write a letter to Asha after considering the following questions: What will you say to her? Should you call her Asha or Bhavi? What is your mood and should you reveal it to her?

D. The Shoe on the Other Foot

Imagine that Asha has invited her friend to move in with Deepak and her. But she has not consulted Deepak to get his opinion. This friend plans to stay for a year, maybe longer. Write a paragraph describing how Deepak will react to the news that Asha's friend is moving in. Write a second paragraph describing how you think he should react.

E. She's Sorry, but Then Again . . .

> [Asha] listened as a part of herself cried out to her to go to [Deepak], apologize and offer to have Raj back. . . .
>
> Then for the first time she lay down alone in the big bed and let the night cover her slowly.

Asha's loyalties are divided. A part of her wants to apologize, while another part pulls her in another direction. Write a letter to Deepak about Asha. Explain her confusion to him. As you write, answer the following questions: What part of Asha wants to apologize? What do you think the other part of her feels, and why does that part win out? Which part should she listen to?

F. Gender and Culture

"Doors" is written by a woman from India. If the story had been written by a woman from your country, how would Asha and Deepak behave? If a man from your culture had written the story, how would Asha and Deepak behave toward each other? To do this assignment, choose a scene from the story and rewrite it from the point of view of a man or woman from your culture.

Focus on Language

Imagery

Writers often use images to bring their stories and poems to life. Imagery is a special kind of language that uses a word or phrase that excites the reader's senses (sight, hearing, touch, sound, and taste). Such word pictures often appeal more strongly to the reader's emotions than to his or her intellect. Exploring the images that the author uses helps a reader have a greater appreciation and understanding of the story.

Below are four images used by Chitra Divakaruni in "Doors." Read each one carefully. Using the image as a guide, write a description of the picture that you see in your mind. Focus your attention on the italicized words. An example is given below.

> Example: Raj was a *lanky whirlwind.*
> Description of the image: Raj was *tall and thin.* He *never stopped moving,* not even for a minute.

Now write descriptions using the images below.

1. [Deepak and his family] had constantly *spilled* into each others' rooms.

2. Asha stood *frozen* as [Raj's] *sing-song* voice *faded* beyond the bend of the stairs.

_____

3. Raj's eager voice *floated* up to her.

_____

4. [Asha] let the night *cover* her slowly, *layer by cold layer.*

_____

To learn more about South Asian-American culture, consult the materials listed in the "Additional Works of Interest" section.

UNIT 2

"Farewell"
by Liz Sohappy Bahe

Meet the Author

Liz Sohappy Bahe, a Native American who belongs to the Yakima Indian tribe, was born in 1947 near Toppenish, Washington. Her Indian name is Omnama Cheshuts, which means Stopping on a Hill and Looking Down. After spending her childhood in Washington, she attended high school at the Institute of American Indian Arts in Sante Fe, New Mexico. She later returned there to study in a postgraduate poetry workshop.

Preparing to Read

Saying Good-bye

The English language contains many different ways of saying good-bye: "So long" and "bye" are just two of the many expressions that English-speakers use. If you listen to a variety of people as they say good-bye, you will soon realize that the expressions they use vary according to the speaker's age group. One of the first forms of good-bye that Americans teach their small children is "bye-bye." American teenagers like to say good-bye in unusual ways such as "I'm outta here," "See ya," "Catch ya later" or its shortened form "Later," while American adults tend to prefer the more conservative "good-bye" and "bye." Occasionally, Americans will use expressions borrowed from other languages: "Ciao" (pronounced "chow") from Italian and "Adios" from Spanish.

1. With a partner, make a list of other ways you know to say good-bye in English.

   _____

   _____

   _____

2. What are the different ways to say good-bye in your native language?

_____

3. Who uses them?

_____

4. Are some of the expressions used for special occasions?

_____

5. What expressions have been borrowed from other languages?

_____

The First Reading

From the title of the poem, predict what you think the poem is about. Now read the poem once.

Farewell

You sang round-dance songs.
I danced not to thundering drums
but to your voice singing.

You chiseled wood sculpture.
I watched not the tools or chips fly   5
but your strong hands carving.

You lived in a northern village.
I went there not to meet your people
but to walk where you had walked.

You followed calling drums.   10
I waited, willing the drums to stop.

Now write down any thoughts or feelings you have about the poem. Then compare your reactions to the poem with a classmate's reactions. How are your reactions similar to or different from those of your classmate?

A Closer Look

Reread the poem "Farewell." Then write down your answers to the questions below. When you finish, compare your responses to a classmate's. This activity helps you discover what the poem means to you. It also shows how a poem can have more than one meaning.

1. Describe what you think is happening in the poem.

   _____

2. Why do you think the speaker danced to the singing voice and not to the drums?

   _____

3. Why do you think the speaker watched the hands carving instead of the tools or wood?

   _____

4. What do the lines "I went there not to meet your people / but to walk where you had walked" mean to you?

   _____

5. What message do you think the drums called out? Why do you think the speaker "willed" the drums to stop?

   _____

Sharing the Possibilities

Ask your partner the following questions. How do your answers compare with your partner's answers?

1. Do you think the narrator is male or female? What words in the poem helped you decide?

   _____

2. What is the nature of the relationship between the narrator and the "you" of the poem? How did your own experiences as a male or female help you decide?

   _____

3. What kind of culture is described in the poem? In what country do you think the poem takes place?

   _____

4. When you close your eyes and think of the poem, what images (sights and sounds) from the poem remain with you?

   _____

Understanding What a Poem Does

The language of poetry is generally quite different from the language of stories and novels, also known as prose. Poets often choose unusual words and combine them in an unusual way that is very different from everyday language. This special use of language can confuse a reader at first. But with repeated readings, a reader can develop a much deeper understanding of a poem. Read the following poem by Naoshi Koriyama.

Unfolding Bud

One is amazed
By a water-lily bud
Unfolding
With each passing day,
Taking on a richer color
And new dimensions.

5

One is not amazed,
At first glance,
By a poem,
Which is as tight-closed   10
As a tiny bud.

Yet one is surprised
To see the poem
Gradually unfolding,
Revealing its rich inner self,   15
As one reads it
Again
And over again

How is a poem like a water lily? Do you agree or disagree with Koriyama's idea that, as we read a poem, it reveals itself to us? Explain your answer.

The words of a poem help shape readers' thoughts and feelings. When readers read a poem, they react to it emotionally, intellectually, even physically. They may cry because the words of the poem evoke sad memories, or they may smile because the words amuse them. By using their imaginations, readers can even see, hear, taste, smell, and touch the images described in the poem. But not everyone reacts to a poem in the same way. In fact, many times one reader will like a poem that another reader dislikes.

Why do you think readers react differently to the same poem?

Extending the Reading Experience

Choose one of the following activities to complete.

1. Rewrite the poem from the viewpoint of the singer in "Farewell."
2. Draw or paint a picture that shows your personal interpretation of the poem.
3. Turn the poem into a short story. Write at least one paragraph for each stanza.

Focus on Language

Characteristics of a Poem

Authors use their imaginations to create short stories, novels, and poems. All three types of literature invite readers to explore their own thoughts and feelings. Poems, though, are different from short stories and novels in several ways.

First, poems are usually quite short by comparison. The lines of a poem are typically arranged as a narrow column of words on the page. They are also frequently grouped into "paragraphs" called *stanzas*.

1. Look at the poem called "Farewell." Notice how the author uses space. Identify the *lines* of the poem as well as the *stanzas*.
2. Next, compare the poem "Farewell" with the short story "Doors." Notice the difference in how the two authors use space.

Second, poets have traditionally used rhyme to help express their ideas. Listen to your teacher read the following English *limerick* by Edward Lear.

> There is a young lady whose nose
> Continually prospers and grows;
> When it grew out of sight, she exclaimed in
> a fright,
> "Oh! Farewell to the end of my nose!"

Notice that certain words share the same vowel and consonant sounds: nose/grows; sight/fright. This sound pattern is known as rhyme. Notice also that these rhyming words fall at the ends of clauses. Not all poetry contains such obvious rhyme patterns. In fact, much modern poetry contains very

little or no rhyme. This kind of poetry is called *open form* verse (at one time called free verse).

Look again at "Farewell." Does it contain any obvious rhyme?

In addition to rhyme, the limerick above also contains a very obvious rhythm. In English, a rhythmic pattern is created using *syllables* and accent or *stress.* A stressed syllable sounds louder than the syllables around it. The combination of loud and soft (quiet) syllables creates a pattern of sounds. Traditional poetry contains obvious sound patterns—a regular rhythm, like the drumbeat of a song. This kind of poetry is known as *closed form.* On the other hand, a poem written in open form frequently lacks an obvious pattern of sound—it contains an irregular rhythm, an irregular beat.

Listen again to your teacher read Lear's limerick. Underline the syllables that are stressed (sound louder) or try clapping to the beat.

Reread "Farewell." Do you detect a regular or an irregular rhythmic pattern? Compare your answer to a classmate's answer.

Finally, rather than use rhythmic patterns like the one in Lear's limerick, a poet might repeat certain phrases and words throughout a poem. Like the rhythm of a song, this repetition of words and phrases can be reassuring and pleasant sounding for the reader. Once a pattern is established, however, poets sometimes change the pattern in order to surprise their readers. "Farewell" is an example of a poem that contains repetition.

Circle the key words that are repeated in "Farewell." Compare your answers with a classmate's answers.

See the "Additional Works of Interest" section for a list of books, sound recordings, and videos about Native American culture.

UNIT 3

"La Puerta"
by José Antonio Burciaga

Meet the Author

Born in 1940, José Antonio Burciaga was an artist, writer, and humorist of international renown. From 1985 to 1994, he served as a resident fellow at Stanford University. While at Stanford he painted many of the murals at the student dorm Casa Zapata. His publications include two collections of his essays, *Spilling the Beans: Lotería Chicana* and *Drink Cultura: Chicanismo,* and also a book of poetry, *Undocumented Love,* a 1992 American Book Award winner. José Burciaga died in 1996.

Preparing to Read

"Necessity Knows No Frontiers"

Whether they are rich, poor, or middle class, people from around the world want a good life for themselves and their families. For the poor, this usually means food, a safe home, and medical care—what most people would call the simple necessities of life. However, these basic necessities are sometimes impossible luxuries for the poor, who may not experience even the simple pleasure of a full stomach. To feed and clothe their families, many of the world's poor must make great sacrifices, even leaving their families in order to make a living in another country. Many come to the United States.

In the 1980s, approximately six million legal immigrants entered the United States. Forty-four percent were from Asia, while 40 percent came from Mexico and other Latin American countries (Griffin 1992). During the same ten-year period, millions of immigrants entered the United States illegally. Approximately 55 percent of these immigrants came from Mexico (372). They had crossed the U.S.-Mexican border, risking their lives in the hopes of finding employment in the United States. At the same time, many U.S. citizens complained that illegal immigrants from Mexico took jobs away from U.S. citizens and put a strain on U.S. social services. In response to this outcry, the U.S. government announced plans in 1992 to improve the lighting and fencing along the U.S.-Mexican border as well as to add another three hundred border patrol agents (369). In spite of efforts to stop the flow of illegal immigrants from Mexico, many Mexicans continue to enter the United States illegally every year. Most of these immigrants cross the border to escape the poverty of their homeland, but fewer than 10 percent remain in the United States permanently—most return home to Mexico (374).

In your homeland, what hardships do the poor face in order to feed, clothe, and shelter their families?

_____

_____

The First Reading

From the title of the story, "La Puerta" (The Door), what do you think the story is about? Why call the story "La Puerta"? A "door" to where? Try reading the entire story without stopping to use your dictionary.

La Puerta

It had rained in thundering sheets every afternoon that summer. A dog-tired Sinesio returned home from his job in the mattress sweat shop. With a weary step from the *autobús*,[1] Sinesio gathered the last of his strength and darted across the busy *avenida*[2] into the ramshackle *colonia*[3] where children played in the meandering pathways that would soon turn into a noisy *arroyo*[4] of rushing water. The rain drops striking the *barrio's*[5] tin, wooden and cardboard roofs would soon become a sheet of water from heaven.

Every afternoon Sinesio's muffled knock on their two-room shack was answered by Faustina, his wife. She would unlatch the door and return to iron more shirts and dresses of people who could afford the luxury. When thunder clapped, a frightened Faustina would quickly pull the electric cord, believing it would attract lightning. Then she

---

1. *autobús*—bus
2. *avenida*—avenue
3. *colonia*—neighborhood
4. *arroyo*—stream
5. *barrio*—neighborhood

would occupy herself with preparing dinner. Their three children would not arrive home for another hour.

On this day Sinesio laid down his tattered lunch bag, a lottery ticket and his week's wages on the oily tablecloth. Faustina threw a glance at the lottery ticket.

Sinesio's silent arrival always angered Faustina so she glared back at the lottery ticket, "Throwing money away! Buying paper dreams! We can't afford dreams, and you buy them!"

Sinesio ignored her anger. From the table, he picked up a letter, smelled it, studied the U.S. stamp, and with the emphatic opening of the envelope sat down at the table and slowly read aloud the letter from his brother Aurelio as the rain beat against the half tin, half wooden rooftop.

5

Dear Sinesio,

I write to you from this country of abundance, the first letter I write from *los Estados Unidos*.[6] After two weeks of nerves and frustration I finally have a job at a canning factory. It took me that long only because I didn't have the necessary social security number. It's amazing how much money one can make, but just as amazing how fast it goes. I had to pay for the social security number, two weeks of rent, food, and a pair of shoes. The good pair you gave me wore out on our journey across the border. From the border we crossed two mountains, and the desert in between.

I will get ahead because I'm a better worker than the rest of my countrymen. I can see that already and so does the "boss." Coming here will be hard for you, leaving Faustina and the children. It was hard enough for me and I'm single without a worry in life. But at least you will have me here if you come and I'm sure I can get you a job. All you've heard about the crossing is true. Even the lies are true. "*Saludos*"[7] from your "*compadres*"[8] Silvio and Ramiro. They are doing

---

6. *los Estados Unidos*—the United States
7. *Saludos*—Greetings
8. *compadres*—good friends

fine. They're already bothering me for the bet you
made against the Dodgers.

Next time we get together I will relate my
adventures and those of my "*compañeros*"[9] . . .
things to laugh and cry about.

Aurelio signed the letter *Saludos y abrazo.*[10] Sinesio   10
looked off into space and imagined himself there already.
But this dreaming was interrupted by the pelting rain and
Faustina's knife dicing nopal, cactus, on the wooden
board.

¿Qué crees?—"What do you think?" Faustina asked
Sinesio.

¡No sé!—"I don't know," Sinesio responded with
annoyance.

"But you do know, Sinesio. How could you not know?
There's no choice. We have turned this over and around a
thousand times. That miserable mattress factory will
never pay you enough to eat with. We can't even afford the
mattresses you make!"

Sinesio's heart sank as if he was being pushed out or
had already left home. She would join her *comadres*[11] as
another undocumented widow. Already he missed his
three children, Celso, Jenaro, and Natasia his eldest, a joy
every time he saw her. "An absence in the heart is an
empty pain," he thought.

Faustina reminded Sinesio of the inevitable trip with   15
subtle statements and proverbs that went straight to the
heart of the matter. "Necessity knows no frontiers," she
would say. The dicing of the nopal and onions took on the
fast clip of the rain. Faustina looked up to momentarily
study a trickle of water that had begun to run on the
inside of a heavily patched glass on the door. It bothered
her, but unable to fix it at the moment she went back to
her cooking.

Sinesio accepted the answer to a question he wished
he had never asked. The decision was made. There was no

---

9. *compañeros*—companions
10. *Saludos y abrazo*—Greetings and an embrace
11. *comadres*—good friends (female)

turning back. "I will leave for *el norte*[12] in two weeks," he said gruffly and with authority.

Faustina's heart sank as she continued to make dinner. After the rain, Sinesio went to help his *compadre* widen a ditch to keep the water from flooding in front of his door. The children came home, and it became Faustina's job to inform them that Papá would have to leave for a while. None of them said anything. Jenaro refused to eat. They had expected and accepted the news. From their friends, they knew exactly what it meant. Many of their friends' fathers had already left and many more would follow.

Throughout the following days, Sinesio continued the same drudgery at work but as his departure date approached he began to miss even that. He secured his family and home, made all the essential home repairs he had put off and asked his creditors for patience and trust. He asked his sisters, cousins and neighbors to check on his family. Another *compadre* lent him money for the trip and the *coyote*.[13] Sinesio did not know when he would return but told everyone "One year, no more. Save enough money, buy things to sell here and open up a *negocio*, a small business the family can help with."

The last trip home from work was no different except for the going-away gift, a bottle of *mezcal*,[14] and the promise of his job when he returned. As usual, the *autobús* was packed. And as usual, the only ones to talk were two loud young men, *sinvergüenzas*—without shame.

The two young men talked about the *Lotería Nacional* 20
and a lottery prize that had gone unclaimed for a week. "¡*Cien millones de pesos!*—One hundred million pesos! ¡*Carajo!*" one of them kept repeating as he slapped the folded newspaper on his knees again and again. "Maybe the fool that bought it doesn't even know!"

"Or can't read!" answered the other. And they laughed with open mouths.

---

12. *el norte*—the north

13. *coyote*—colloquial expression for an American citizen who illegally transports individuals across the U.S.-Mexican border. The coyote collects a fee for the transport and is often abusive.

14. *mezcal*—colorless Mexican liquor

This caught Sinesio's attention. Two weeks earlier he had bought a lottery ticket. "Could . . . ? No!" he thought. But he felt a slight flush of blood rush to his face. Maybe this was his lucky day. The one day out of the thousands that he had lived in poverty.

The two jumped off the bus, and Sinesio reached for the newspaper they had left behind. There, on the front page, was the winning number. At the end of the article was the deadline to claim the prize: 8 that night.

Sinesio did not have the faintest idea if his ticket matched the winning number. So he swung from the highest of hopes and dreams to resigned despair as he wondered if he had won one hundred million pesos.

Jumping from the bus, he ran home, at times slowing   25
to a walk to catch his breath. The times he jogged, his heart pounded, the newspaper clutched in his hand, the heavy gray clouds ready to pour down.

Faustina heard his desperate knock and swung the door open.

"*¿Dónde está?*"[15] Sinesio pleaded. "Where is the lottery ticket I bought?" He said it slowly and clearly so he wouldn't have to repeat himself.

Faustina was confused, "What lottery ticket?"

Sinesio searched under the table, under the green, oily cloth, on top of the dresser and through his papers, all the while with the jabbing question, "What did you do with the *boleto de lotería?*"[16]

Thunder clapped. Faustina quit searching and   30
unplugged the iron. Sinesio sounded off about no one respecting his papers and how no one could find anything in that house. *¿Dónde está el boleto de lotería?*—Where is the lottery ticket?

They both stopped to think. The rain splashed into a downspout against the door. Faustina looked at the door to see if she had fixed the hole in the glass.

¡La puerta!—"The door!" blurted Faustina, "I put it on the door to keep the rain from coming in!"

Sinesio turned to see the ticket glued on the broken window pane. It was light blue with red numbers and the

---

15. *¿Dónde está?*—Where is it?
16. *boleto de lotería*—lottery ticket

letters "*Lotería Nacional.*" Sinesio brought the newspaper up to the glued lottery ticket and with his wife compared the numbers off one by one—*Seis - tres - cuatro - uno - ocho - nueve - uno - ¡SIETE - DOS!*[17]—Sinesio yelled.

"No!" trembled a disbelieving and frightened Sinesio, "One hundred million pesos!" His heart pounded afraid this was all a mistake, a bad joke. They checked the numbers again and again only to confirm the matching numbers.

Sinesio then tried to peel the numbers off. His fingernails slid off the cold, glued lottery ticket. Faustina looked at Sinesio's stubby fingernails and moved in. But Faustina's thinner fingernails also slid off the lottery ticket. Sinesio walked around the kitchen table looking, thinking, trying to remain calm.   35

Then he grew frustrated and angry. "What time is it?"

"A quarter to seven," Faustina said, looking at the alarm clock above the dresser. They tried hot water and a razor blade with no success. Sinesio then lashed out at Faustina in anger, "You! I never answered your mockery! Your lack of faith in me! I played the lottery because I knew this day would come! "*¡Por Dios Santo!*" and he swore and kissed his crossed thumb and forefinger. "And now? Look what you have done to me, to us, to your children!"

"We can get something at the *farmacia!*[18] The doctor would surely have something to unglue the ticket."

"*¡Sí! ¡O sí!*"[19] mocked Sinesio. "Sure! We have time to go there."

Time runs faster when there is a deadline. The last bus downtown was due in a few minutes. They tried to take the broken glass pane off the door but he was afraid the ticket would tear more. Sinesio's fear and anger mounted with each glance at the clock.   40

In frustration, he pushed the door out into the downpour and swung it back into the house, cracking the molding and the inside hinges. One more swing, pulling,

17. *Seis - tres - cuatro - uno - ocho - nueve - uno - ¡SIETE - DOS!*—Six - three - four - one - eight - nine - one - SEVEN - TWO!
18. *farmacia*—pharmacy, drugstore
19. *¡Sí! ¡O sí!*—Yes! Oh yes!

twisting, splintering, and Sinesio broke the door completely off.

Faustina stood back with hands over her mouth as she recited a litany to all the *santos*[20] and virgins in heaven as the rain blew into their home and splashed her face wet.

Sinesio's face was also drenched. But Faustina could not tell if it was from the rain or tears of anger, as he put the door over his head and ran down the streaming pathway to catch the autobús.

Closer Look

Immediately after finishing the story, respond in writing to the following questions on the lines provided. (Read the story again if you need to.) Then share your responses with a classmate.

1. When you close your eyes, what images (mental pictures) remain with you as a result of reading the story? Describe your mental pictures.

---

20. *santos*—saints

2. What memories, if any, does the story awaken in you?

_____

3. What part of the story did you find especially interesting, sad, funny, and so on? Why was this part special to you?

_____

4. What part of the story did you find confusing or disturbing?

_____

Sharing the Possibilities

1. Using your answer to the third question—"What part of the story did you find especially interesting, sad, funny, and so on?"—create two questions you would like answered about that part of the story.

_____

_____

2. Using your answer to the fourth question—"What part of the story did you find confusing or disturbing?"—create two questions that you would like answered about that part of the story.

_____

_____

3. Give your four questions to two of your classmates to answer. After they respond to your questions, talk to them about their answers. How are their responses similar to and/or different from one another?

_____

_____

Understanding Characterization

Authors use various ways to describe their characters' personalities. Probably the most commonly used technique is characterization through action. A character's personality is revealed by what he or she does and says. To better understand a character, a reader must look closely at how that character behaves throughout the story. By looking at the character's actions as a whole, a reader can usually surmise the character's beliefs, attitudes, and values.

Look at the following excerpts from the story. Decide what each action "says" or reveals about the character.

> Example: When thunder clapped, a frightened Faustina would quickly pull the electric cord, believing it would attract lightning.

Some readers might think that Faustina's reaction to the thunder is silly and superstitious. Others might say she is very practical and wise. What do you think Faustina's actions say about her?

A. What does each of the following passages reveal about Faustina?
1. Faustina threw a glance at the lottery ticket. Sinesio's silent arrival always angered Faustina so she glared back at the lottery ticket.

   _____

2. Faustina looked up to momentarily study a trickle of water that had begun to run on the inside of a heavily patched glass on the door. It bothered her, but unable to fix it at the moment she went back to her cooking.

   _____

   _____

3. Faustina looked at the door to see if she had fixed the hole in the glass.

   _____

   _____

Now find another passage that helps you understand more about Faustina's personality. Consider *all* of these passages together. Explain to a classmate what you think they reveal about Faustina's personality.

B. What does each of the following passages reveal about Sinesio?
   1. Sinesio ignored [Faustina's] anger. From the table, he picked up a letter, smelled it, studied the U.S. stamp, and with the emphatic opening of the envelope sat down at the table and slowly read aloud.

   _____

   _____

   2. Sinesio looked off into space and imagined himself there [in the United States] already.

   _____

   _____

   3. Sinesio's heart sank as if he was being pushed out or had already left home.

   _____

   _____

Now find another passage in the story that helps you understand more about Sinesio's personality. Consider *all* of these passages together. Explain to a classmate what you think they reveal about Sinesio's personality.

C. Finally, compare Sinesio with Faustina. Are their personalities alike or different? Explain your answer by using your responses to A and B.

Extending the Reading Experience

A. On the Way to the Autobús

   Time runs faster when there is a deadline. The last bus downtown was due in a few minutes. . . .
   [Sinesio] put the door over his head and ran down the streaming pathway to catch the autobús.

   1. And so the story ends. But what happens to Sinesio next?!! Imagine that you are Sinesio running down the street, stepping over rain puddles, perhaps slipping in the mud and even attracting the neighborhood dogs. All the while you are carrying the door (la puerta) over your head. With only minutes to spare, do you catch

the autobús? Make a list of the obstacles you meet on your way to claim your one hundred million pesos. Explain to a classmate how Sinesio would deal with these obstacles.

2. Again imagine that you are Sinesio. A day has passed since you went to the lottery office. Using your list of obstacles, write a letter to your brother Aurelio describing in detail what happened to you on your way to the lottery office. Finish the letter below, which has been started for you.

```
Dear Aurelio,
     You won't believe what happened to me yesterday!
```

B. **Her Heart Sank**

The children came home, and it became Faustina's job to inform them that Papá would have to leave for a while.

1. Imagine that you are Faustina. Your three children are seated at the kitchen table, quietly waiting for your explanation. What do you say to them to help them understand that "necessity knows no frontiers"?

2. Imagine that you are one of Faustina and Sinesio's three children. What would be your greatest fear about your father's going to the United States? What questions would you ask your mother?

C. *Lotería Nacional*—A Scenario

Assume that Sinesio has arrived at the lottery office in time to claim his winnings. He rushes into the lottery office with the door held above his head. All eyes stare at him. As Sinesio struggles to regain his breath, a small pool of muddy water collects at his feet. What happens next?

Divide into two groups. One group will represent the lottery official; the other will represent Sinesio. Each group will prepare a "plan of action" for its character to follow. Using these plans of action, two "actors," chosen by the groups, will portray Sinesio and the official.

Instead of writing dialogue for the actors to memorize and recite, each group will suggest a variety of ways that its scenario actor can respond to the other actor. In this way, the scenario is more like real life—in real life, we can only guess how other people will behave; we can never know for certain. To ensure that the scenario will be spontaneous and natural, keep your group's plan of action a secret.

Group 1. *The Lottery Official*
Decide what the lottery official might say and do when Sinesio, dripping wet, steps up to the counter carrying a door over his head. It is also very important for your group to anticipate the many different ways that Sinesio might act. You must also consider the different things Sinesio might say. With this in mind, decide how the lottery official could respond to him. Choose one person from the group to be the lottery official. Remember to keep your plan a secret.

Group 2. *Sinesio*
Decide what Sinesio might say and do when he is confronted by the official. You must also anticipate what the lottery official might say and do. Will the official be confused, angry, amused? With the lottery official in mind, decide how Sinesio might behave. Choose one person from the group to be Sinesio. Remember to keep your plan a secret.

The two actors should now enact the scene based on the groups' discussions. Remember that the "acting" should be unrehearsed and spontaneous.

Focus on Language

Action Verbs

To make their stories more appealing, writers frequently use action verbs. Rather than describing abstract ideas, action verbs describe activities that can be seen—*running* and *jumping* are examples of action verbs. These special verbs help readers create a vivid mental picture of a character's physical behavior. Burciaga uses many such verbs to help readers "see" his characters in action.

Following are sentences that contain eight action verbs taken from "La Puerta."

A. Write a description of the action expressed by each underlined verb.

Example: Faustina *diced* the nopal.
diced—to cut something (vegetables, fruit, meat) into small pieces using very quick, short knife strokes.

1. Sinesio *darted* across the busy avenue.

2. He *slapped* the newspaper on his knee again and again.

_____

3. Sinesio *clutched* the newspaper in his hand.

_____

4. He *trembled* as he read the numbers on the lottery ticket.

_____

5. Sinesio tried to *peel* the ticket off the window.

_____

6. His fingernail *slid* off the slippery ticket.

_____

7. Sinesio *twisted* the door from its hinges.

_____

B. Divide into groups of four. Write the eight words on slips of paper—one word per slip. Put the slips into a hat or bag. Each person then picks out two slips of paper. Do not show the verbs to each other. Take turns pantomiming the verbs' actions. The group members must guess what verb is being acted out.

Literal Language

Words that describe real events and objects are called literal language. The sentence "The bird flew through the air" describes a concrete or real event. We can say that the bird literally flew through the air. That is, it is something that we can actually see.

The eight action verbs listed in exercise A are examples of literal language because they describe real or concrete actions. The characters literally dice, dart, slap, and so on. As concrete verbs they are very easily expressed through pantomime.

Below are four more sentences that contain words that describe actions. These words can also be pantomimed. In these sentences, the words' meanings are literal. In other words, they describe something that is concrete.

C. With a partner, define the literal or concrete meanings of the italicized words. Then pantomime the action that they express.

Example: Her purse *swung* from her arm as she walked down the street.
Definition: to move back and forth with a regular motion

Pantomime by moving your arm back and forth with a regular motion.

1. He was a real troublemaker. He enjoyed *jabbing* other children with his ballpoint pen.
   Definition: _____
   Pantomime the action.
2. She *threw* the baseball to her daughter.
   Definition: _____
   Pantomime the action.
3. The teacher quickly *gathered* his books and papers from his desk.
   Definition: _____
   Pantomime the action.

Figurative Language

Another form of descriptive language is called *figurative language*. It describes something that is abstract, an idea for instance. The English idiom "Time flies" expresses an abstract concept. Time doesn't really fly away like a bird—it just seems to fly sometimes, especially when we are busy.

In exercise C, you looked at the literal meanings of four words (*swing, jab, throw,* and *gather*). Although these words can describe real or concrete actions, their meanings can also be figurative. That is, in certain contexts these same words can describe abstract ideas.

D. With a partner, read the sentences below. Then answer the questions
   that follow to help you determine the figurative meanings of the italicized words. Notice how each italicized word still keeps some of its literal meaning.

   Example: Sinesio *swung* from the highest of hopes and dreams to
      resigned despair.
   What does it mean to "swing" from high hopes to despair?
   Answer—emotions move back and forth from the highest of hopes to
      the lowest despair.

   1. He searched under the table, all the while with the *jabbing* ques-
      tion, "What did you do with the lottery ticket?"
      How can a question be "jabbing"? Why would someone ask a jab-
      bing question? How would a jabbing question sound?

      _____

   2. Faustina *threw* a glance at the lottery ticket.
      What does it mean to "throw" a glance? What would this look like?

      _____

   3. Sinesio *gathered* the last of his strength.
      What does it mean to "gather" one's strength? Gather from where?

      _____

See the "Additional Works of Interest" section for a list of books, sound
recordings, and videos about Mexican-American culture.

UNIT 4

"Jobs" by Wendy Wilder Larsen and Tran Thi Nga

Meet the Authors

In 1970 Wendy Wilder Larsen moved from the United States to Vietnam to be with her husband, a journalist covering the Vietnam War, and to teach Shakespeare and romantic poetry at the University of Saigon. While in Saigon, Larsen met Tran Thi Nga, who was the bookkeeper in Larsen's husband's office. Before long they became friends. Acting as a guide to life in Saigon, Nga helped Larsen understand the Vietnamese culture in which she now found herself immersed. In 1971 Wendy Larsen returned to the United States, leaving behind her friend and a culture she had come to know. Then in 1975, just days before Saigon fell to the communists, Nga escaped the city and came to the United States, where she contacted her old friend. Their friendship grew deeper as they talked about old times and new. They decided that such stories were worth recording. Out of their collaboration came a collection of poems about their experiences, *Shallow Graves: Two Women and Vietnam,* from which "Jobs" is taken.

Preparing to Read

Today's Immigrant

In the nineteenth century and the first half of the twentieth century, immigrants from Asia and Europe were principally farmers and unskilled laborers, often poorly educated and illiterate (Min 1995, 16). In contrast, the latter half of the twentieth century has seen a significant change in the educational and occupational characteristics of immigrants. Primarily from urban and middle class backgrounds, recent immigrants to the United States tend to be much better educated than earlier immigrants. In fact, most post-1965 Asian immigrants have a much higher educational level than both the U.S. general population and other immigrant groups. From 1985–90, 40.7 percent of all Asian immigrants to the United States had college degrees earned in their countries of origin, with the Philippines leading the way (17–18). However, despite being college graduates, many immigrants from all countries have experienced difficulty finding professional jobs in the United States.

1. Name three reasons why immigrants might have difficulty finding jobs in their fields.

    _____

    _____

    _____

2. Name three ways immigrants can increase their chances of getting a good job in the United States.

    _____

    _____

    _____

3. Make a list of jobs you would not like to do. What makes each one undesirable?

    _____

    _____

    _____

4. Now make a list of ideal jobs. What makes each of these jobs attractive?

    _____

    _____

    _____

The First Reading

As you read the poem, be aware of any thoughts and feelings that you are having. Pay special attention to the jobs that are described and the people who work them. Remember that stopping to use a dictionary during the first reading will slow you down.

Jobs

We took the jobs available,
My son-in-law, who had a law degree,
sold the Electrolux vacuum cleaner
demonstrated door to door.
American people are afraid of Asians.   5
They would not let him in.

My sons worked as mechanics,
sold gasoline at night for extra money
until they were robbed.
My daughter worked in a training program   10
for a cosmetics company.
Bao and my sister started a small grocery store
near the university, selling notebooks, cigarettes,
cookies, ice cream, newspapers for the students.

My brother is an electrician.   15
My daughter-in-law stayed home
to cook and watch the babies.
We all studied English at night.
One of our friends in Saigon
was Chief Justice of the Supreme Court.   20
He was trained in France
spoke four languages.
He wrote me:
"I am a watchman in Houston.
When they hired me,   25
they felt uneasy with my title,
called me a telephone operator.
When anyone knocks on the door
of the company, I open it.
They call me a telephone operator,   30
but to tell you the truth,
I am a watchman."

From what I have seen in the States,
education means less than in my country.
There, if you are well educated,   35
you are sure of a high position and respect.

We say with the Chinese,
"Learn to handle a writing brush
and you will not handle a begging bowl."
Here a skilled worker makes a lot of money.   40
America is an industrial society.

Reread the poem. Which of the jobs mentioned in the poem would you find the *least* attractive? Why?

A Closer Look

Make a list of the jobs that are described in the poem. If necessary, read "Jobs" again. Then compare your list to a classmate's list. Together decide which jobs require higher education, which require special schooling, and which require neither.

Sharing the Possibilities

Answer the following questions on separate paper. Then share your answers with your classmates and teacher.

1. In the first stanza, the authors write, "American people are afraid of Asians. They would not let [my son-in-law] in." Do you agree that Americans are fearful of Asians? Explain. Why would they be afraid? Can you think of other reasons why the Americans would not let the young man in? How would you feel if you were this young man?

2. In the second stanza, the sons worked as mechanics, the daughter worked for a cosmetics company, and Bao and his wife opened a grocery store. Why do you suppose they took these jobs? Do you believe they felt satisfied? Why or why not?

3. Look at the third stanza. What is so ironic about the fate of the friend from Saigon? What does a "watchman" do? Why do you think his company insists on calling him a "telephone operator" instead of a "watchman"?

4. In the final stanza, the authors state, "From what I have seen in the States, education means less than in my country. There, if you are well educated, you are sure of a high position and respect." Does education mean less in the United States than in *your* country? Explain.

Understanding Poetic Meaning

Poet Matthew Arnold once said that poetry should embody a "criticism of life." In other words, poets try to shed light on the human experience by closely examining or "criticizing" life. In the process, they help readers to better understand the human condition and human emotions: joy, frustration, fear, love, among others. Readers see their own lives and the lives of others reflected in poetry. It is this personal reflection and the promise of a better understanding of life that draw us to poetry.

1. Look again at "Jobs." In your opinion, what is the *critical message* about *working* in the United States? About *education* in the United States? How is your own experience working in the United States, or the experiences of people you know, reflected in the poem? Write your answers on paper. Then share them with a classmate.
2. Larsen and Nga focus on *jobs* for their critical message. Other topics that would lend themselves to a criticism of life include *marriage, family, money, war, the status of women or children, and government.* On the lines below, add to this list of "critical" topics. Choose topics that are important to you. Keep in mind that criticism is not always negative. It simply means an honest, sometimes painful, look at life. Share your list with a classmate.

_____

_____

_____

Extending the Reading Experience

Authors use examples to help them make a point. Look again at the list of jobs you made for "A Closer Look." These concrete examples of the job situations of friends and relatives of one of the authors of the poem support a critical message about working in the United States. Also notice how the poem builds up to the strong *extended* example of the former chief justice of the supreme court. Look again at this extended example. How does it strengthen the message you see in the poem?

1. Choose one of the topics you listed for "Understanding Poetic Meaning." Pick the topic that is most important to you. What *critical message* would you like to tell about this topic? Write the topic on a piece of paper. Underneath the topic, write a sentence that expresses your message about the topic.
2. Next make a list of concrete examples that support your topic and illustrate your critical message. Your examples can be drawn from your own life and/or from the lives of people you have known, observed, or read about. Which of your examples could be extended to strengthen your message?

Focus on Language

Authors often use proverbs to express meaning because proverbs are believed to express certain undeniable truths about life. "Jobs" contains a Chinese/Vietnamese proverb: "Learn to handle a writing brush and you will not handle a begging bowl." Do you think this proverb speaks the truth? How is its meaning related to the rest of the poem? Does your country have a similar proverb?

Using your topic and list of examples from "Extending the Reading Experience," write a poem or essay that expresses your "criticism of life." Important: use a proverb from your country that supports your critical message.

For a list of books, sound recordings, and videos about the Vietnamese-American culture, consult the "Additional Works of Interest" section.

UNIT 5

"The Circuit"
by Francisco Jiménez

Meet the Author

Francisco Jiménez was born in the small village of San Pedro Tlaquepaque, Mexico. When he was four years old, his parents brought the family across the border to seek work in the United States. Because of his poor understanding of English, Francisco was held back in the first grade. But he persisted, overcame tremendous obstacles, and graduated from high school, earning three college scholarships. He received his M.A. and Ph.D. in Spanish and Latin American literature from Columbia University. Today Dr. Francisco Jiménez is Professor of Modern Languages and the associate vice president for academic affairs at Santa Clara University. He has also authored, coauthored, and edited numerous books ranging from literary criticism to collections of contemporary Latino writing. In 1997, he published *The Circuit: Life of a Migrant Child,* a collection of semiautobiographical short stories about children in migrant agricultural life.

Preparing to Read

Migrant Farmworkers

America's agricultural industry owes much of its good fortune to the thousands of migrant workers who labor in fields, orchards, and vineyards. Following the growing season of America's food crops, migrants move from farm to farm in search of work. Across the United States, many migrant workers are Chicano (Mexican-American). Oranges, grapefruit, grapes, strawberries, and lettuce are just a few of the many kinds of produce that Chicano migrant laborers harvest by hand. Men, women, and children work side by side in the fields. Many of the children regularly miss school in order to work in the fields.

The farmwork that these migrants do is often as dangerous as it is difficult. Heat, dust, and insecticides threaten the health of these workers. In addition to enduring poor working conditions, migrants and their families must frequently tolerate miserable living conditions. Farm owners normally provide places for migrants and their families to live, but these places are often dirty and rundown. Despite the hardships that are a part of their daily existence, many migrants are able to maintain close-knit families. Keeping the family together is as important as finding the next season's work.

Nomadic Lifestyles—Past and Present

Many people around the world lead nomadic or seminomadic lifestyles; that is, they travel from place to place—hunting wild animals, gathering wild food, or as is usually the case, searching for food for their livestock to eat. Like many migrant workers, nomads do not have permanent homes or addresses. For example, before the twentieth century, many American Indians (American Indians are also known as Native Americans) led the life of nomads. Because they followed the herds of wild animals as they roamed across the countryside, the nomadic tribes never settled in one place for very long.

Think of your own culture for a moment. What groups of people lead nomadic lifestyles in your country today? What groups led nomadic lifestyles in the past?

_____

_____

Modern society does not support or encourage nomadic lifestyles. For instance, to qualify for such services as public schooling, health insurance, and government assistance, a person living in America typically needs a permanent home address. With this in mind, what kinds of problems do you think a migrant family would encounter in the United States?

_____

_____

The First Reading

Look at the title of the story. What does the word *circuit* mean? Now read "The Circuit" once without stopping. For unfamiliar words, use the context of the words rather than your dictionary.

The Circuit

It was that time of year again. Ito, the strawberry sharecropper, did not smile. It was natural. The peak of the strawberry season was over and the last few days the workers, most of them *braceros,*[1] were not picking as many boxes as they had during the months of June and July.

As the last days of August disappeared, so did the number of braceros. Sunday, only one—the best picker—came to work. I liked him. Sometimes we talked during our half-hour lunch break. That is how I found out he was from Jalisco, the same state in Mexico my family was from. That Sunday was the last time I saw him.

When the sun had tired and sunk behind the mountains, Ito signaled us that it was time to go home. "*Ya esora,*"[2] he yelled in his broken Spanish. Those were the words I waited for twelve hours a day, every day, seven days a week, week after week. And the thought of not hearing them again saddened me.

As we drove home Papá did not say a word. With both hands on the wheel, he stared at the dirt road. My older brother, Roberto, was also silent. He leaned his head back and closed his eyes. Once in a while he cleared from his throat the dust that blew in from outside.

Yes, it was that time of year. When I opened the front door to the shack, I stopped. Everything we owned was neatly packed in cardboard boxes. Suddenly I felt even more the weight of hours, days, weeks, and months of work. I sat down on a box. The thought of having to move to Fresno and knowing what was in store for me there brought tears to my eyes.

That night I could not sleep. I lay in bed thinking about how much I hated this move.

A little before five o'clock in the morning, Papá woke everyone up. A few minutes later, the yelling and screaming of my little brothers and sisters, for whom the move

5

---

1. *braceros*—Mexican farmworkers who came to the United States shortly after World War II as a result of an arrangement made between the U.S. and Mexican governments.
2. *Ya esora (Ya es hora)*—It's time to quit.

was a great adventure, broke the silence of dawn. Shortly, the barking of the dogs accompanied them.

While we packed the breakfast dishes, Papá went outside to start the "Carcanchita." That was the name Papá gave his old '38 black Plymouth. He bought it in a used-car lot in Santa Rosa in the winter of 1949. Papá was very proud of his little jalopy. He had a right to be proud of it. He spent a lot of time looking at other cars before buying this one. When he finally chose the "Carcanchita," he checked it thoroughly before driving it out of the lot. He examined every inch of the car. He listened to the motor, tilting his head from side to side like a parrot, trying to detect any noises that spelled car trouble. After being satisfied with the looks and sounds of the car, Papá then insisted on knowing who the original owner was. He never found out from the car salesman, but he bought the car anyway. Papá figured the original owner must have been an important man because behind the rear seat of the car he found a blue necktie.

Papá parked the car out in front and left the motor running. "*Listo,*"[3] he yelled. Without saying a word, Roberto and I began to carry the boxes out to the car. Roberto carried the two big boxes and I carried the two smaller ones. Papá then threw the mattress on top of the car roof and tied it with ropes to the front and rear bumpers.

Everything was packed except Mamá's pot. It was an old large galvanized pot she had picked up at an army surplus store in Santa Maria the year I was born. The pot had many dents and nicks, and the more dents and nicks it acquired the more Mamá liked it. "*Mi olla,*"[4] she used to say proudly.

I held the front door open as Mamá carefully carried out her pot by both handles, making sure not to spill the cooked beans. When she got to the car, Papá reached out to help her with it. Roberto opened the rear car door and Papá gently placed it on the floor behind the front seat. All of us then climbed in. Papá sighed, wiped the sweat off his forehead with his sleeve, and said wearily: "*Es todo.*"[5]

10

---

3. *Listo*—Ready
4. *Mi olla*—My pot
5. *Es todo*—All done, all finished

As we drove away, I felt a lump in my throat. I turned around and looked at our little shack for the last time.

At sunset we drove into a labor camp near Fresno. Since Papá did not speak English, Mamá asked the camp foreman if he needed any more workers. "We don't need no more," said the foreman, scratching his head. "Check with Sullivan down the road. Can't miss him. He lives in a big white house with a fence around it."

When we got there, Mamá walked up to the house. She went through a white gate, past a row of rose bushes, up the stairs to the front door. She rang the doorbell. The porch light went on and a tall husky man came out. They exchanged a few words. After the man went in, Mamá clasped her hands and hurried back to the car. "We have work! Mr. Sullivan said we can stay there the whole season," she said, gasping and pointing to an old garage near the stables.

The garage was worn out by the years. It had no windows. The walls, eaten by termites, strained to support the roof full of holes. The dirt floor, populated by earth worms, looked like a gray road map.

15

That night, by the light of a kerosene lamp, we unpacked and cleaned our new home. Roberto swept away the loose dirt, leaving the hard ground. Papá plugged the holes in the walls with old newspapers and tin can tops. Mamá fed my little brothers and sisters. Papá and Roberto then brought in the mattress and placed it on the far corner of the garage. "Mamá, you and the little ones sleep on the mattress. Roberto, Panchito, and I will sleep outside under the trees," Papá said.

Early next morning Mr. Sullivan showed us where his crop was, and after breakfast, Papá, Roberto, and I headed for the vineyard to pick.

Around nine o'clock the temperature had risen to almost one hundred degrees. I was completely soaked in sweat and my mouth felt as if I had been chewing a handkerchief. I walked over to the end of the row, picked up the jug of water we had brought, and began drinking. "Don't drink too much; you'll get sick," Roberto shouted. No sooner had he said that then I felt sick to my stomach. I dropped to my knees and let the jug roll off my hands. I remained motionless with my eyes glued to the hot sandy ground. All I could hear was the drone of insects. Slowly I began to recover. I poured water over my face and neck and watched the dirty water run down my arms to the ground.

I still felt a little dizzy when we took a break to eat lunch. It was past two o'clock and we sat underneath a large walnut tree that was on the side of the road. While we ate, Papá jotted down the number of boxes we had picked. Roberto drew designs on the ground with a stick. Suddenly I noticed Papá's face turn pale as he looked down the road. "Here comes the school bus," he whispered loudly in alarm. Instinctively, Roberto and I ran and hid in the vineyards. We did not want to get in trouble for not going to school. The neatly dressed boys about my age got off. They carried books under their arms. After they crossed the street, the bus drove away. Roberto and I came out from hiding and joined Papá. "*Tienen que tener cuidado*,"[6] he warned us.

After lunch we went back to work. The sun kept beating down. The buzzing insects, the wet sweat, and the hot dry dust made the afternoon seem to last forever. Finally the mountains around the valley reached out and swallowed the sun. Within an hour it was too dark to continue picking. The vines blanketed the grapes, making it difficult to see the bunches. "*Vámonos*,"[7] said Papá, signaling to us that it was time to quit work. Papá then took out a pencil and began to figure out how much we had earned our first day. He wrote down numbers, crossed some out, wrote down some more. "*Quince*,"[8] he murmured.

20

When we arrived home, we took a cold shower underneath a waterhose. We then sat down to eat dinner around some wooden crates that served as a table. Mamá had cooked a special meal for us. We had rice and tortillas with "*carne con chile*,"[9] my favorite dish.

The next morning I could hardly move. My body ached all over. I felt little control over my arms and legs. This feeling went on every morning for days until my muscles finally got used to the work.

---

6. *Tienen que tener cuidado*—You have to be careful.
7. *Vámonos*—Let's go.
8. *Quince*—Fifteen
9. *carne con chile*—spicy meat

It was Monday, the first week of November. The grape season was over and I could now go to school. I woke up early that morning and lay in bed, looking at the stars and savoring the thought of not going to work and of starting sixth grade for the first time that year. Since I could not sleep, I decided to get up and join Papá and Roberto at breakfast. I sat at the table across from Roberto, but I kept my head down. I did not want to look up and face him. I knew he was sad. He was not going to school today. He was not going tomorrow, or next week, or next month. He would not go until the cotton season was over, and that was sometime in February. I rubbed my hands together and watched the dry, acid-stained skin fall to the floor in little rolls.

When Papá and Roberto left for work, I felt relief. I walked to the top of a small grade next to the shack and watched the "Carcanchita" disappear in the distance in a cloud of dust.

Two hours later, around eight o'clock, I stood by the side of the road waiting for school bus number twenty. When it arrived I climbed in. Everyone was busy either talking or yelling. I sat in an empty seat in the back.

25

When the bus stopped in front of the school, I felt very nervous. I looked out the bus window and saw boys and girls carrying books under their arms. I put my hands in my pants pockets and walked to the principal's office. When I entered I heard a woman's voice say: "May I help you?" I was startled. I had not heard English for months. For a few seconds I remained speechless. I looked at the lady who waited for an answer. My first instinct was to answer her in Spanish, but I held back. Finally, after struggling for English words, I managed to tell her that I wanted to enroll in the sixth grade. After answering many questions, I was led to the classroom.

Mr. Lema, the sixth grade teacher, greeted me and assigned me a desk.

He then introduced me to the class. I was so nervous and scared at that moment when everyone's eyes were on me that I wished I were with Papá and Roberto picking cotton. After taking roll, Mr. Lema gave the class the assignment for the first hour. "The first thing we have to do this morning is finish reading the story we began yesterday," he said enthusiastically. He walked up to me, handed me an English book, and asked me to read. "We are on page 125," he said politely. When I heard this, I felt my blood rush to my head; I felt dizzy. "Would you like to read?" he asked hesitantly. I opened the book to page 125. My mouth was dry. My eyes began to water. I could not begin. "You can read later," Mr. Lema said understandingly.

For the rest of the reading period I kept getting angrier and angrier with myself. I should have read, I thought to myself.

During recess I went into the restroom and opened my   30
English book to page 125. I began to read in a low voice, pretending I was in class. There were many words I did not know. I closed the book and headed back to the classroom.

Mr. Lema was sitting at his desk correcting papers. When I entered he looked up at me and smiled. I felt better. I walked up to him and asked if he could help with the new words. "Gladly," he said.

The rest of the month I spent my lunch hours working on English with Mr. Lema, my best friend at school.

One Friday during lunch hour Mr. Lema asked me to take a walk with him to the music room. "Do you like music?" he asked me as we entered the building.

"Yes, I like *corridos*,"[10] I answered. He then picked up a trumpet, blew on it and handed it to me. The sound gave me goose bumps. I knew that sound. I had heard it in many corridos. "How would you like to learn how to play it?" he asked. He must have read my face because before I could answer, he added: "I'll teach you how to play it during our lunch hours."

That day I could hardly wait to get home to tell Papá   35
and Mamá the great news. As I got off the bus, my little brothers and sisters ran up to meet me. They were yelling and screaming. I thought they were happy to see me, but when I opened the door to our shack, I saw that everything we owned was neatly packed in cardboard boxes.

---

10. *corridos* —traditional Mexican ballads

A Closer Look

As you read for another time, be aware of any questions and/or thoughts and feelings that occur to you. Stop reading long enough to record your thoughts on paper. Ask yourself: "What feelings am I having as I read? Does the story remind me of any past experiences I've had, any people I've known, or any places I've seen? Does this story remind me of any other stories I have read or movies I have seen?" Also, how does the title reflect the events in the story?

Sharing the Possibilities

Answer the following questions by recording your ideas on a sheet of paper.

1. What single event in the story had the greatest emotional impact on you? Why do you think it had this effect?
2. Describe the family in "The Circuit." What kind of relationship do the family members seem to have with each other? How is this relationship reflected in the characters' words and actions?
3. When Panchito returns home from school at the end of the story, he finds that his family is preparing to leave the Sullivan farm. Change the ending of the story to your liking. Would you need to change the title as well?

Exchange papers with a classmate. Did you both choose the same event for question 1? Did you have similar emotional reactions? Or are your answers to question 1 different? Compare your description of the family with your classmate's. Do you both view the family in the same light? Or does one of you see the positive nature of the family's relationship while the other focuses on the negative? How do your revised ending and title compare with your classmate's choices of ending and title?

Chances are you and your classmate responded differently to all of the questions, especially questions 1 and 3. Why do you think this would happen?

Understanding Point of View

Before they begin to write, fiction writers must ask themselves, "Who will tell my story?" That is, who will be the storyteller or narrator of the story? From whose point of view will the story be told? Will it be an unnamed person who remains outside of the story's action. This kind of narrator usually acts like an objective reporter. To achieve this type of "objective" narration, the author uses the third person point of view. But what if one of the characters is telling the story? In that case, the author uses the first person point of view to indicate who is telling the story. Look closely at "The Circuit." Who's telling the story—someone *outside* the story or one of the characters?

Changing Point of View

If we change a story's point of view, we change the course of the story. The following activities help you understand how changing point of view can alter a story.

1. The following event is told from the point of view of Panchito. Imagine for a moment that you are Roberto sitting across the breakfast table from Panchito, your little brother. As Roberto, what are you feeling? What are you thinking? How are you acting? Retell this same event from the point of view of Roberto.

   Since I [Panchito] could not sleep, I decided to get up and join Papá and Roberto at breakfast. I sat at the table across from Roberto, but I kept my head down. I did not want to look up and face him. I knew he was sad. He was not going to school today. He was not going tomorrow, or next week, or next month. He would not go until the cotton season was over, and that was sometime in February.

2. The following event is told from Panchito's point of view. Imagine that you are Mr. Lema, Panchito's sixth grade teacher. If you were Mr. Lema, the teacher, what would you be feeling, thinking, and doing? Retell the same event from Mr. Lema's point of view.

> After taking roll, Mr. Lema gave the class the assignment for the first hour. "The first thing we have to do this morning is finish reading the story we began yesterday," he said enthusiastically. He walked up to me, handed me an English book, and asked me to read. "We are on page 125," he said politely. When I heard this, I felt my blood rush to my head; I felt dizzy. "Would you like to read?" he asked hesitantly. I opened the book to page 125. My mouth was dry. My eyes began to water. I could not begin. "You can read later," Mr. Lema said understandingly.

Extending the Reading Experience

In Words and Pictures

Imagine that you are part of a journalistic team for a major newspaper in your home country. The team is made up of investigative reporters and graphic artists. Your boss has sent the team to the Sullivan vineyard in Fresno, California, to record in words and pictures the lifestyles of American migrant workers. Choose one of the following assignments to complete.

A. On the plane to Fresno, you remember that your boss wants a vivid description of the migrants' living conditions on the Sullivan farm. As soon as you arrive at the Sullivan place, you visit with several of the migrant families in their homes. What do you see, hear, and smell? What do the family members tell you? How do they act? Review paragraphs 15, 16, and 21 for ideas but use your imagination, too. *In your own words,* write a multiparagraph article that describes the *people* and the *living conditions* on the Sullivan farm. Give your article a title that will catch your readers' attention.

B. Your newspaper has made you an undercover investigative reporter. This means that you will go to the Sullivan farm pretending to be a migrant worker. Mr. Sullivan needs more workers; therefore, he hires you without hesitation. While at the farm, you investigate working conditions in the vineyard. What do you experience as a worker picking grapes? What do the workers around you experience? Review paragraphs 18, 19, and 20 but use your imagination, too. *In your own words,* write a multiparagraph article in which you describe the *working conditions* that you find. "Hook" your readers with an interesting title.

C. As the newspaper's graphic artist, you've been assigned the task of drawing or painting a picture that captures the hardships and hopes of the migrant people. Your boss has given you a choice of *one* of the following assignments: Draw or paint freehand or use a computer to create one of the following: (1) a portrait of one of the migrant workers or family members; (2) a picture of where a family lives; or (3) a sketch of the migrants at work in the fields. Then write a paragraph describing your picture. Your boss has offered you a bonus if you draw all three subjects and write a paragraph about each one.

Interviews

Your editor wants to include a human interest story—that is, an in-depth article about one migrant. Alone, or with one or two other people, complete the following assignment.

Step One—"Interview" one of the four characters described below. After each name is a short passage about the character. Using this passage and your understanding of the character, write down three questions you want to ask this person. Next imagine how your character would answer these three questions. Write these answers beneath your questions.

1. Mamá

> Everything was packed except Mamá's pot. It was an old large galvanized pot she had picked up at an army surplus store in Santa Maria the year I was born. The pot had many dents and nicks, and the more dents and nicks it acquired the more Mamá liked it.

2. Papá

> "Carcanchita." That was the name Papá gave his old '38 black Plymouth. He bought it in a used-car lot in Santa Rosa in the winter of 1949. Papá was very proud of his little jalopy. . . . Papá fig-

ured the original owner must have been an important man because behind the rear seat of the car he found a blue necktie.

3. Roberto

I [Panchito] sat at the table across from Roberto, but I kept my head down. I did not want to look up and face him. I knew he was sad. He was not going to school today. He was not going tomorrow, or next week, or next month. He would not go until the cotton season was over.

4. Mr. Lema

Mr. Lema was sitting at his desk correcting papers. When I entered he looked up at me and smiled. I felt better. I walked up to him and asked if he could help me with the new words. "Gladly," he said.

The rest of the month I spent my lunch hours working on English with Mr. Lema, my best friend at school.

Step Two—What does the character from step one look like in your imagination? How would you describe his or her personality? Write a paragraph describing the character's personality and physical characteristics. Finally, share your human interest story with your classmates. How do your descriptions differ?

A Compilation of Student Work
Create a class anthology of student articles. First, neatly recopy or type your investigative report and your interview, making revisions and corrections as necessary. Then divide the class into two teams (in the case of a large class, divide into four or more teams to create more than one anthology). One team should gather all of the students' articles and pictures together, put them into logical order, and then create a table of contents. The other team should design a cover that reflects the assignment and the class's individuality. (If your school has the resources, have a copy of the anthology made for each student.) Finally, securely bind the materials.

Focus on Language

Transitions in Narratives

Events in narratives are usually presented in chronological order, that is, according to real time. To make the sequence of time both obvious and natural, authors use time words—words and phrases that signal specific times of the day, week, and year as well as the passage of time such as day to night, season to season, even year to year.

The passage of time seems to be an especially important element in "The Circuit." Following are just a few of the many phrases that signal the movement of time in the story.

that time of year again
the last few days
during the months of June and July
the last days of August
our half-hour lunch break
for twelve hours a day, every day, seven days a week, week after week
that night
before five
a few minutes later

With a partner, search the story for additional phrases that help make the reader aware of the passage of time. How many of these phrases can you find?

To learn more about Mexican-American culture, see the list of materials in the "Additional Works of Interest" section.

UNIT 6

"The Purchase"
by Nick C. Vaca

Meet the Author

Nicolas C. Vaca is currently an attorney in California, where he is a principal in the law firm of Vaca, Vaca, & Ritter in Walnut Creek, California. Nicolas Vaca received his J.D. from Harvard Law School and his B.A., M.A., and Ph.D. from the University of California at Berkeley. He continues to write fiction while practicing law, and he published a short story in the April 1997 issue of the *California Lawyer*.

Preparing to Read

Prejudgment

Prejudice means prejudging, that is, drawing a conclusion about someone or something without first discovering the facts about that person or object or event. The primary causes of prejudice are misunderstanding and ignorance. Very often feelings of prejudice result in acts of discrimination, even violence. People who think they are racially, culturally, even physically superior will often treat others with suspicion. For example, a person of one race, culture, religion, or gender may mistrust, even hate, another person simply because he or she is different.

Recall a time when you or someone you know was prejudged. Describe the incident to a classmate. Where did it take place? Who was involved? What happened? How can prejudice be eliminated?

The First Reading

Read "The Purchase" without stopping. As you read, resist the temptation to use your dictionary.

The Purchase

"*Ave Maria Purísma,*[1] I must make another *pago hoy*[2] or else it'll be too late. Sí, too late, and then what would I do? Christmas is so close, and if I don't hurry *con los pagos,*[3] I'll have nothing to give any of *mis hijos.*[4] If that happens, it would weigh *muy pesado*[5] on my mind. Even now, *con el pensamiento*[6] that I may not be able to give them anything, I have trouble *durmiendo en la noche.*[7] And, Santo Niño do Atocha, if Christmas should come and catch me *sin nada,*[8] I would never sleep well *por el resto de mi vida.*"[9]

Sitting on a large, bulky sofa, its brown cover worn and frayed at the arm rests and back, Doña Lupe was thinking over the progress she had made in her Christmas shopping. Surrounded by the wrinkles of her small, sad face, two dark eyes closed and opened intermittently as her gray head nodded in deep absorption, figuring the amount of time and money she needed to complete her shopping. Becoming agitated with pleasure and anxiety, she lifted her thin body off the sofa, wrapped her faded green sweater around her waist, and began shuffling[10] from one end of the three-room apartment to the other as she tightly pursed her lips and placed her fingers on her sunken cheeks, again losing herself in a world of calculations. As she reached the far end of the apartment, she stopped at the bay window, gathered her arms about herself, and dropped her head slightly to one side. Outside the sky was a cold gray with the dark clouds and fog combining to form low, dark shadows that covered Stockton as far as Doña Lupe could see. Below her apartment an elm

---

1. *Ave Maria Purísma*—Hail Mary most pure
2. *pago hoy*—payment today
3. *con los pagos*—with the payments
4. *mis hijos*—my children
5. *muy pesado*—very heavy
6. *con el pensamiento*—with the thought
7. *durmiendo en la noche*—sleeping in the night
8. *sin nada*—without anything
9. *por el resto de mi vida*—for the rest of my life
10. shuffling—sliding one's feet along

tree with morning dewdrops still fresh on its naked branches began to sway slightly as the first gush of cold morning wind disturbed its somnolent serenity,[11] causing Doña Lupe to shiver slightly. Shuffling to the kitchen table, she sat down and pulled a grease-spotted piece of brown paper out of her apron pocket. Clearing the salt shaker, a bowl of *chile salsa,* and some cold tortillas that remained from last evening's dinner, Doña Lupe placed the paper on the table. As she squinted under the light of the naked light bulb that hung directly overhead, her fingers underlined names and Xs on the paper. The names were those of her children, and the Xs indicated who had been bought a gift. The names were meaningless. That is, they meant a great deal to her, but she did not know them. Doña Lupe could not read. But she had memorized them in the order that they appeared on the paper after Antonio, her youngest son, read them over and over to her during the past two months; so now, even if she didn't know how to read, she knew for whom the various scrawlings[12] stood. The list began with Gilbert, her eldest son, and ended with Gloria, her youngest daughter, and everyone but Rudy, who was in the army, had the large, dark, trembling X of her black grease pencil.

Had anyone told Doña Lupe five years ago when her husband died that she would be able to buy store gifts for her children, she would have shaken her head in polite disagreement. Her monthly welfare allowance only covered the necessities that life imposed on her—the rent of her apartment, her food, clothing, and her weekly movie at the Mexican movie house every Saturday with Doña Pifora, another widow who met her necessities in the same manner. To even think that she would be able to buy store gifts for her children was very much out of the question. As Doña Lupe reasoned, either she had to come into a lot of money, or she would have to buy on credit. The chances of her coming into a lot of money did not even occupy her thoughts, and credit, well, that was something that only people with money could afford. So she contented herself

---

11. serenity—quietness, peacefulness
12. scrawlings—careless handwriting

with giving her daughters colorfully embroidered[13] dish towels, and inexpensive handkerchiefs to her sons. That's the way it had been for the past five years, ever since her husband's death, when a lack of money and friends had driven her to her apartment and her daily existence. And so it would have probably continued until her death, had she not sighed during one of her Saturday movie dates with Doña Pifora.

"Ay, Doña Pifora, Christmas is coming again, and I have to start making *mis hijos* something again. I'm getting tired of giving them the same thing year after year. I know they don't mind my presents, but I do. You know how it is; you have *hijos* of your own; it's not like you're ignorant of the matter."

Doña Pifora nodded in agreement.   5

"It's difficult to explain," continued Doña Lupe, "but when you don't give your *hijos* anything for Christmas, you don't feel good inside. My *hijos* tell me that it doesn't matter, that I shouldn't even think about giving gifts to so many of them. They say it's silly what I do every year, but I still feel bad if I can't give them anything for Christmas. Christmas is special, and special times shouldn't go unnoticed."

"Well," inquired Doña Pifora, "why don't you give them gifts from the store? They're right, you know. It's too much what you do for them each year," added Doña Pifora cautiously.

"Why?" answered Doña Lupe. "You know that all my money, every bit of it, is used *en la casa*.[14] For food, *la renta*, some clothing, things like that. That's why. I don't have money to go around buying store presents."

"Of course you do," countered Doña Pifora; "everybody does. Listen, it's clear you haven't heard of lay-away," Doña Pifora declared so loudly that several people in the foyer of the theater turned and looked at them.

"Lay-away, *¿qué es eso?*"[15] inquired Doña Lupe.   10

"It's like credit," proceeded Doña Pifora, "but not really credit. That is, it works almost the same. What you do is this. You go to a store that has lay-away and look around.

---

13. embroidered—decorated with needlework
14. *en la casa*—at home
15. *¿qué es eso?*—what is that?

If you find something you like, you just take it to the
counter and tell the lady you want to buy it, but that you
don't have enough money and that you would like it put
on lay-away. Then you give the lady fifty cents or whatever
you have. Then every week or when you have money, you
give them what you can. The only thing is that you can't
have the thing you want until you pay for it."

"What?" asked Doña Lupe.

"Oh, *sí;* until you finish the payments, you can't have
it," answered Doña Pifora.

"Well, that's not too bad, I guess," said Doña Lupe.
"After all, it's only fair that they should keep the things
until you finish paying for them. It's the only right thing to
do."

"Where do they have this lay-away, Doña Pifora?"   15
inquired Doña Lupe.

"Well, I always do my lay-away at Clifford's; you know,
the store on the big street with the large trees across from
the big hotel," answered Doña Pifora.

"Clifford's, eh?" added Doña Lupe softly, almost to herself.

Though Doña Lupe feigned[16] a mild interest in the lay-
away plan, her heart was beating furiously with excitement at the prospect that for the first time in five years
she would have a chance to give her children some store-
bought presents. What she had told Doña Pifora about
needing all her money was true. But for store gifts she
would sacrifice a little. Perhaps she didn't have to eat as
well, not buy clothes for a while, and give up her Saturday
movies. That would be the most painful sacrifice, but she
would do it.

It was a cold and windy October morning when Doña
Lupe set out for Clifford's, a dollar in her apron pocket
and a head full of dreams. As she shuffled past children
playing in the park, the autumn leaves swirled about her
feet, and the crisp morning air foretold the coming of winter. Clifford's was a variety store of the sort that sold
almost anything, and the anything it sold was generally of
poor quality. It was to this store that most of the pension-
ers and mothers on welfare came to buy their clothing,
ironing boards, sweets, and the other necessities that the

---

16. feigned—pretended

corner grocery store could not provide. In short, it was the type of store that can be found in almost any small town in the San Joaquin Valley. Catering to the poor and aged, Clifford's reflected its attitude to its clientele[17] in the arrangement and treatment of its goods. Shoes were thrown in with plastic balls, Orlon sweaters were placed alongside cans of paint; potted plants were surrounded by greeting cards, and the floor was unswept. The clerks were generally fresh out of high school, and even if they worked at Clifford's for years, they still looked as if they were fresh out of high school. They chewed gum as they arranged items on counters and engaged in conversation with each other as they waited on customers. The boys would shoulder each other as they worked in pairs along the aisles. The young girls would constantly pat their hair to ensure its perfection.

Ambling along the aisles looking cautiously at items, even daring to touch and examine them, Doña Lupe attempted to settle in her mind that the explanation Doña Pifora had made of the lay-away was both real and accurate, and what she saw could be hers. Whatever doubts she had about the existence of lay-aways were dispelled[18] by the sense of exhilaration[19] that she could own what she saw. Her eyes moved rapidly, selecting items with her eyes tightened to cover the smile that strove to break through all her restraint. For Ruth she chose a black porcelain cat with diamond eyes that sparkled nicely when they were held against the light; for Felicia she chose a bouquet of plastic flowers; for Antonio she chose a gold colored chain; for Antonia she chose a porcelain collie dog, and so it went until all ten children had been selected presents. Cradling them in her arms, she carefully placed them one by one on the counter as the clerk, a girl of about eighteen years with pimples and heavy make-up, began to examine them. Before the girl could begin totaling the items, the words *lay-away* slipped from Doña Lupe's mouth. The young girl's forehead furrowed.[20]

"What?" she said.

20

---

17. clientele—customers
18. dispelled—made to disappear
19. exhilaration—excitement
20. furrowed—wrinkled

"Lay-away," blurted Doña Lupe.

"Oh yeah, wait a minute, huh," mumbled the girl.

Turning towards the back of the store, the girl shouted, "Oh, Mr. Clifford, this Mexican woman wants this stuff on lay-away."

From behind the candy counter a tall man, with thin-ning hair, wire-rim glasses, a large straight nose, and a pale, colorless face approached Doña Lupe.   25

"Want this stuff on lay-away, huh?" he asked.

"Lay-away," repeated Doña Lupe. Her English was lim-ited, but she felt that lay-away was all the man needed to know. If such a thing existed, she knew it would be self-explanatory. If it didn't exist, it was no use trying to explain how it worked, especially if she had to refer to Doña Pifora. Because if lay-away didn't exist, then how would he know about Doña Pifora?

"Yeah, all right," said the tall man in a resigned tone.

The items, all of them, totaled twenty-five dollars. Writ-ing out a receipt for the items, the tall man placed them in a cardboard box, taped the receipt on the box, and placed it underneath the counter; then he turned to Doña Lupe and said, "How much you gonna put down?"

Doña Lupe reached into her apron pocket and pulled   30
out the crumpled dollar she had saved in the last week and placed it on the counter.

"Just one dollar. That all you gonna put down?" inquired the man.

Doña Lupe nodded her head.

"Well, if that's all you got, that's all you got," said the tall man philosophically as he placed the dollar in the cash register.

"You know the deal," continued the tall man; "come in every week and give a dollar or whatever you got to give, and when you finish paying the twenty-five dollars, then you get the stuff. Okay?"

Doña Lupe nodded her head and shuffled out the door   35
happy that the October wind was cold, the sun bright, and that the winter was on its way.

That had occurred two months ago, or as Doña Lupe counted, eight payments ago. Now all she had left to pay was $6.43, and today was the ninth week of her pay-ments. This week she planned to pay three dollars, which she had saved by . . . well, modesty hoards[21] that secret, and next week she planned to pay the remaining amount. As she reached the kitchen table for the fifth time in her pacing, Doña Lupe stopped and noticed that the clock showed eight. She put on her heavy coat, placed a black scarf on her head, and stepped into the dull December day with the fog still hanging low and the houses and trees shivering in the damp morning. The thought that this was the second to the last payment gave her a feeling of modest satisfaction that even such a sad morning could not dispel. As was now the custom, when she made her payments, she was usually the only customer at such an early hour. Following her usual routine, she located the tall man in the back of the store and paid her three dollars; but instead of leaving the store as was her usual fashion, she lingered along the aisles looking and holding things that caught her attention—plastic flowers, small, furry dogs that squealed when squeezed and made Doña Lupe smile, sweaters, velvet ribbons. Having satisfied her curiosity, she slowly shuffled out the door. As she began crossing the street, her right arm was grabbed and a nervous but firm voice said, "All right, lady, what you got?"

Doña Lupe turned to see a tall, redheaded boy wearing the familiar green smock that all Clifford's employees were made to wear. The boy could not have been over seventeen years, and his young face showed a combination of determination and confusion. Doña Lupe was dumbfounded.[22]

"Yeah, don't act dumb; what you got? What's under the coat? I know it's there. You weren't walking around for so long for nothing. I had my eye on you. Come on, now; what is it? We get your kind all the time. Walk around acting dumb and then pinch something like nothing happened."

Flustered[23] from embarrassment and hurt at the thought that she should be accused of stealing, Doña Lupe simply stared at the young man. In her sixty-eight years of life she had never stolen a thing, and to be

---

21. hoard—hide
22. dumbfounded—shocked
23. Flustered—Nervous

accused of such an act was the most horrible thing she could imagine. She held herself stiffly.

"All right; since you're not gonna talk, then let's see   40
what you got."

The young man flung open her coat to find that she had stolen nothing. A sheepish[24] grin came over his face; he muttered something and quickly went inside.

Doña Lupe could not bear the thought of being accused of stealing. She wept quietly all the way home. Arriving at her apartment, she took off her coat but left her scarf on and began to pace the floor again. It was one o'clock in the morning when she finally stopped pacing, sat down on the brown sofa, and began embroidering dish towels.

Closer Look

Reread the story. Stop occasionally to record your thoughts on paper, then continue reading. Ask yourself: "What feelings am I having as I read? Does the story remind me of any past experiences I've had, any people I've known, or any places I've visited?"

---

24. sheepish—embarrassed

Sharing the Possibilities

Written Conversations

During this activity, you will write a letter to your partner about the story. You and your partner should follow the exercise below. Before you start, decide who will be Student A and who will be Student B.

Student A

1. Write a letter to your partner describing your reactions to "The Purchase." You can record your opinions, write down some questions for your partner to answer, tell how the story makes you feel, and so on. Write nonstop for five to ten minutes.
2. When you have finished writing, give your letter to your partner.

Student B

1. While your partner is writing, look again at the story. Have any of your opinions about the story changed?
2. Then read your partner's letter as soon as he or she gives it to you.
3. Next respond to your partner's comments by writing him or her a letter. Which of your partner's opinions do you agree with/disagree with? Write some questions for your partner to answer. Express your own feelings about the story. Write nonstop for five to ten minutes.

Student A

1. While your partner is responding to your letter, look again at the story. Have any of your opinions about the story changed?
2. When your partner gives you his or her written comments, respond to them in writing. Again write for five to ten minutes.

Continue your "letter writing" until each of you has responded in writing three times.

Understanding Setting and Mood

Authors place characters and plot (action) inside a *setting*. Setting can be divided into four elements.

1. Physical locale (country, village, city, indoors, outdoors, bedroom, kitchen, etc.)
2. Time (day, year, century, present, past, future)
3. Environmental conditions (hot, cold, sunny, rainy, dusty, sounds, smells, etc.)
4. Social conditions (social and economic class, customs, traditions)

These elements combine to help the reader create the feeling of reality—real place, real time, real conditions—in which the characters "live." These elements also affect the reader's state of mind, evoking moods or emotions such as sadness, joy, solemnity, loneliness, and so forth. Below is a list of words and phrases from the story that describe physical locale and time.

Physical Locale—Stockton (small town), Doña Lupe's apartment (a large, bulky sofa, its brown cover worn and frayed), Clifford's (the floor was unswept), the streets (autumn leaves swirled past her feet)
Time of Year—autumn, October, (dull) December

Complete the exercise below by finding as many words and phrases in the story as you can that describe the environmental conditions in the story.

Environmental Conditions

Example: cold gray sky

_____

_____

_____

_____

Authors use setting to create the feeling of reality. They also use setting to create a mood or an atmosphere (a general or an overall emotion). Look again at your list of words and phrases describing the environmental conditions in "The Purchase." Combine your list with four or five other students' lists. Together decide what moods or emotions the words create.

Extending the Reading Experience

Complete one of the following activities.

1. Write a second chapter to the story. (Check with your teacher about length.) In your sequel will Doña Lupe return to the store or stay away? If she returns to the store, what will she say to Mr. Clifford and the redheaded boy, and how will she act? If she stays away from the store, what will she tell her friend Doña Pifora and her children? In your second chapter, include a description of the setting (see "Understanding Setting and Mood" in this unit). What mood does your setting create? What do your characters say to one another?

2. Write a paper describing a setting that creates a strong feeling (e.g., sorrow, joy, fear, grief, etc.). However, in your paper you cannot name the emotion. Instead let your detailed descriptions of the physical locale, the time of year, and the environmental conditions create the emotion. When you have finished your paper, ask a classmate and your teacher to read it and then guess what mood or emotion you had in mind.

3. Based on your understanding of the story, describe how poor people like Doña Lupe spend their lives in the United States. In your description, explain why you think the redheaded boy accused Doña Lupe of stealing.

Focus on Language

Idioms

An idiom is an expression that is peculiar to a language and often does not have a literal meaning. Some idioms are quite colorful, defying literal translation. For example, the idiom "to hit the wall" does not refer to the action of running against a wall. It is an idiom that means to exhaust your physical and mental energy as in "Rosa spent night after night cramming for her bar exams until she finally *hit the wall.*" Rosa became exhausted.

With a partner, decide what each idiom means. Then rewrite each sentence without using the idiom. Change the verb forms where necessary. The first one is done for you.

Example: Marie *has had her eye on* Tomas for some time now.
Marie *has been very interested in* Tomas for some time now.

1. The young man knew it was morally and legally wrong to *pinch* something from his neighbor.

   _____

2. Louis wasn't sure how to act around girls since he was *fresh out of* an all-boys school.

   _____

3. Can you go to the store for me? We're *fresh out of* milk.

   _____

4. I've always wanted to be a professional dancer, but unfortunately I have *two left feet.*
   I know what you mean. I've always wanted to be a brain surgeon, but I'm *all thumbs.*

   _____

   _____

5. I'm really surprised to see your brother in Calculus II.
   Me too. He passed Calculus I *by the skin of his teeth.*

   _____

6. Boris was late for dinner again. He said he had to work late.
   Really? Yesterday it was traffic. Last week it was a meeting. Are you sure he's not *feeding you a line?*

   _____

7. You're still doing your hair? The movie starts in just fifteen minutes! Come on. *Shake a leg.*

   _____

8. I'm sorry about yesterday. I didn't mean to yell at you.
   I was pretty nasty myself. Let's *bury the hatchet,* OK?

   _____

9. My brother got an A in Biology II.
   No way! You're *pulling my leg.* I was sure he'd *bite the dust* in that class.

   _____

   _____

10. Mr. Herra is a great teacher. He always *bends over backwards* to help his students learn physics.

    _____

11. When I came home three hours past my curfew, my dad *hit the ceiling.* He told me either *shape up or ship out.*

    _____

    _____

12. I don't know what's *eating* my brother. He yelled at everyone today. Even little things irritate him. He must have *gotten up on the wrong side of the bed* this morning.

    _____

    _____

13. Why is Natalya so happy today?
    She just bought a new car. Normally it's very expensive, but the dealer is going out of business, so she *got it for a song.*
    I just hope it's not a *lemon.* That dealer is not very honest, I hear.

    _____

    _____

14. I was just elected president of the International Student Club, and I joined three other campus organizations.
    Aren't you also a full-time student and a waiter at the Italian restaurant? I think maybe you've *bitten off more than you can chew.* Don't you think you might be *spreading yourself too thin?* I really don't think you can do all that.
    Hey, I can handle it. *Don't sell me short.*

    _____

    _____

    _____

Do you know any other English idioms?
Do you ever use any of these idioms yourself? Share them with your classmates.

See the "Additional Works of Interest" section for a list of books, sound recordings,
and videos about Mexican-American culture and related topics.

UNIT 7

"Wilshire Bus"
by Hisaye Yamamoto

Meet the Author

Born 1921 in Redondo Beach, California, Hisaye Yamamoto began writing at age fourteen for Japanese-American newspapers. During World War II, her family was interned at the Colorado River Relocation Center (Poston) in Arizona, where she worked on the camp newspaper. Hisaye Yamamoto has had numerous stories and articles published in *Harper's Bazaar, Asian America, Pacific Citizen,* and the *Catholic Worker,* among others. Some of these stories and articles have been collected in *Seventeen Syllables and Other Stories.*

Preparing to Read

A Shameful Reality

On December 7, 1941, the Japanese air force bombed Pearl Harbor, an American naval base in the Pacific, killing and wounding thousands of military personnel and civilians. The immediate response to the attack was shock and an increase in hostility toward Japanese-Americans living in the United States. Suspicion, fear, and racism prevailed and led to tragic results for the Japanese and Japanese-Americans living in the United States. During the spring and summer of 1942, more than 110,000 men, women, and children of Japanese ancestry were forced to leave their homes and businesses and enter ten relocation centers (Smith 1995, 161). They lost their homes, businesses, and personal property. Rather than sell their possessions (many of which were priceless antiques) or leave them for looters, many Japanese-Americans destroyed them. The tens of thousands of Japanese who had worked decades to build businesses and acquire homes saw their houses and stores overrun by vulturelike junk sellers and used-furniture dealers. Despite such harsh treatment, nearly 26,000 Japanese-Americans served in the U.S. armed forces during World War II (342). Many were cited for bravery.

For four decades, the shameful reality of the relocation camps remained largely hidden from public scrutiny. It wasn't until 1988 that the U.S. government offered an apology for the mistreatment and paid partial restitution to the approximately 60,000 surviving Japanese-Americans (the Nisei) who had been confined.

The Good Samaritan

Americans have a long tradition of helping others in need, of comforting and clothing even strangers. We call this "being a Good Samaritan." There are times, though, when it seems as if Americans close their eyes to the problems of others. Why do you suppose this is so? In your culture, do you have a Good Samaritan tradition?

_____

_____

Recall a time when a stranger offered you emotional and/or physical support. What did the stranger do for you? How did this make you feel? And what would you have done if the stranger had not given his or her support?

_____

_____

The First Reading

Read the story quickly, resisting the temptation to look up every word. As soon as you have finished reading, write down any ideas that occur to you about "Wilshire Bus." This activity allows you to freely explore the story and your reactions to it.

Wilshire Bus

Wilshire Boulevard begins somewhere near the heart of downtown Los Angeles and, except for a few digressions scarcely worth mentioning, goes straight out to the edge of the Pacific Ocean. It is a wide boulevard and traffic on it is fairly fast. For the most part, it is bordered on either side with examples of the recent stark architecture which favors a great deal of glass. As the boulevard approaches the sea, however, the landscape becomes a bit more pastoral, so that the university and the soldiers' home there give the appearance of being huge country estates.

Esther Kurouwa got to know this stretch of territory quite well while her husband Buro was in one of the hospitals at the soldiers' home. They had been married less than a year when his back, injured in the war, began troubling him again, and he was forced to take three months of treatments at Sawtelle before he was able to go back to work. During this time, Esther was permitted to visit him twice a week and she usually took the yellow bus out on Wednesdays because she did not know the first thing about driving and because her friends were not able to take her except on Sundays. She always enjoyed the long bus ride very much because her seat companions usually turned out to be amiable,[1] and if they did not, she took vicarious pleasure in gazing out at the almost unmitigated[2] elegance along the fabulous street.

It was on one of these Wednesday trips that Esther committed a grave sin of omission which caused her later to burst into tears and which caused her acute discomfort for a long time afterwards whenever something reminded her of it.

The man came on the bus quite early and Esther noticed him briefly as he entered because he said gaily[3] to the driver, "You robber. All you guys do is take money from me every day, just for giving me a short lift!"

Handsome in a red-faced way, greying, medium of height, and dressed in a dark grey sport suit with a yellow-and-black flowered shirt, he said this in a nice, resonant, carrying voice which got the response of a scattering of titters[4] from the bus. Esther, somewhat amused and classifying him as a somatotonic,[5] promptly forgot about him. And since she was sitting alone in the first regular seat, facing the back of the driver and the two front benches facing each other, she returned to looking out the window.

At the next stop, a considerable mass of people piled on and the last two climbing up were an elderly Oriental

5

---

1. amiable—friendly
2. unmitigated—unending
3. gaily—happily
4. a scattering of titters—a small amount of laughter
5. somatotonic—aggressive personality

man and his wife. Both were neatly and somberly clothed and the woman, who wore her hair in a bun and carried a bunch of yellow and dark red chrysanthemums, came to sit with Esther. Esther turned her head to smile a greeting (well, here we are, Orientals together on a bus), but the woman was watching, with some concern, her husband who was asking directions of the driver.

His faint English was inflected in such a way as to make Esther decide he was probably Chinese, and she noted that he had to repeat his question several times before the driver could answer it. Then he came to sit in the seat across the aisle from his wife. It was about then that a man's voice, which Esther recognized soon as belonging to the somatotonic, began a loud monologue[6] in the seat just behind her. It was not really a monologue, since he seemed to be addressing his seat companion, but this person was not heard to give a single answer. The man's subject was a figure in the local sporting world who had a nice fortune invested in several of the shining buildings the bus was just passing.

"He's as tight-fisted[7] as they make, as tight-fisted as they come," the man said. "Why, he wouldn't give you the sweat of his. . ." He paused here to rephrase his metaphor, ". . . wouldn't give you the sweat off his palm!"

And he continued in this vein, discussing the private life of the famous man so frankly[8] that Esther knew he must be quite drunk. But she listened with interest, wondering how much of this diatribe[9] was true, because the public legend about the famous man was emphatic about his charity. Suddenly, the woman with the chrysanthemums jerked around to get a look at the speaker and Esther felt her giving him a quick but thorough examination before she turned back around.

"So you don't like it?" the man inquired, and it was a moment before Esther realized that he was now directing his attention to her seat neighbor.   10

"Well, if you don't like it," he continued, "why don't you

---

6. monologue—a conversation with oneself
7. tight-fisted—to be selfish with one's money
8. frankly—openly
9. diatribe—a bitter and abusive speech or writing

get off this bus, why don't you go back where you came from? Why don't you go back to China?"

Then, his voice growing jovial, as though he were certain of the support of the bus in this at least, he embroidered[10] on the theme with a new eloquence, "Why don't you go back to China, where you can be coolies[11] working in your bare feet out in the rice fields? You can let your pigtails grow and grow in China. Alla samee, mama, no tickee no shirtee. Ha, pretty good, no tickee no shirtee!"

He chortled[12] with delight and seemed to be looking around the bus for approval. Then some memory caused him to launch on a new idea. "Or why don't you go back to Trinidad? They got Chinks[13] running the whole she-bang in Trinidad. Every place you go in Trinidad . . ."

As he talked on, Esther, pretending to look out the window, felt the tenseness in the body of the woman beside her. The only movement from her was the trembling[14] of the chrysanthemums with the motion of the bus. Without turning her head, Esther was also aware that a man, a mild-looking man with thinning hair and glasses, on one of the front benches was smiling at the woman and shaking his head mournfully in sympathy, but she doubted whether the woman saw.

Esther herself, while believing herself properly   15
annoyed with the speaker and sorry for the old couple, felt quite detached.[15] She found herself wondering whether the man meant her in his exclusion order or whether she was identifiably Japanese. Of course, he was not sober enough to be interested in such fine distinctions, but it did matter, she decided, because she was Japanese, not Chinese, and therefore in the present case immune. Then she was startled to realize that what she was actually doing was gloating over[16] the fact that the drunken man had specified the Chinese as the unwanted.

---

10. embroidered—exaggerated
11. coolies—unskilled laborers originally from Asia; this term can be considered offensive
12. chortle—laugh
13. Chinks—an offensive name for Chinese people
14. trembling—shaking
15. detached—separate
16. gloating over—feeling very satisfied with

Briefly, there bobbled[17] on her memory the face of an
elderly Oriental man whom she had once seen from a
streetcar on her way home from work. (This was not long
after she had returned to Los Angeles from the concentra-
tion camp in Arkansas and been lucky enough to get a
clerical job with the Community Chest.) The old man was
on a concrete island at Seventh and Broadway, waiting for
his streetcar. She had looked down on him benignly as a
fellow Oriental, from her seat by the window, then been
suddenly thrown for a loop by the legend on a large lapel
button on his jacket. I AM KOREAN, said the button.

Heat suddenly rising to her throat, she had felt angry,
then desolate and betrayed. True, reason had returned to
ask whether she might not, under the circumstances,
have worn such a button herself. She had heard rumors of
I AM CHINESE buttons. So it was true then; why not I AM
KOREAN buttons, too? Wry, she wished for an I AM
JAPANESE BUTTON, just to be able to call the man's
attention to it, "Look at me!" But perhaps the man didn't
even read English, perhaps he had been actually threat-
ened, perhaps it was not his doing—his solicitous children
perhaps had urged him to wear the badge.

Trying now to make up for her moral shabbiness,[18]
she turned toward the little woman and smiled at her
across the chrysanthemums, shaking her head a little to
get across her message (don't pay any attention to that
stupid old drunk, he doesn't know what he's saying, let's
take things like this in our stride). But the woman, in turn
looking at her, presented a face so impassive[19] yet cold,
and eyes so expressionless yet hostile,[20] that Esther's
overture fell quite flat.

Okay, okay, if that's the way you feel about it, she
thought to herself. Then the bus made another stop and
she heard the man proclaim ringingly, "So clear out, all of
you, and remember to take every last one of your slant-
eyed pickaninnies[21] with you!" This was his final advice as

---

17. bobble—emerged, arose, or appeared suddenly
18. shabbiness—unfairness or poor quality
19. impassive—without emotion
20. hostile—angry, mean
21. pickaninny—offensive name for an African-American child

he stepped down from the middle door. The bus remained at the stop long enough for Esther to watch the man cross the street with a lightly exploring step. Then, as it started up again, the bespectacled[22] man in front stood up to go and made a clumsy speech to the Chinese couple and possibly to Esther, "I want you to know," he said, "that we aren't all like that man. We don't all feel the way he does. We believe in an America that is a melting pot of all sorts of people. I'm originally Scotch and French myself." With that, he came over and shook the hand of the Chinese man.

"And you, young lady," he said to the girl behind Esther, "you deserve a Purple Heart[23] or something for having to put up with that sitting beside you."

   20

Then he, too, got off.

The rest of the ride was uneventful and Esther stared out the window with eyes that did not see. Getting off at last at the soldiers' home, she was aware of the Chinese couple getting off after her, but she avoided looking at them. Then, while she was walking towards Buro's hospital very quickly, there arose in her mind some words she had once read and let stick in her craw: People say, do not regard[24] what he says, now that he is in liquor. Perhaps it is the only time he ought to be regarded.

These words repeated themselves until her saving detachment was gone every bit and she was filled once again in her life with the infuriatingly helpless, insidiously sickening sensation of there being in the world nothing solid she could put her finger on, nothing solid she could come to grips with, nothing solid she could sink her teeth into, nothing solid.

When she reached Buro's room and caught sight of his welcoming face, she ran to his bed and broke into sobs that she could not control. Buro was amazed because it was hardly her first visit and she had never shown such weakness before, but solving the mystery handily,[25] he patted her head, looked around smugly at his roommates,

---

22. bespectacled—wearing eyeglasses
23. Purple Heart—a medal given to a soldier for bravery
24. regard—pay attention to
25. handily—easily

and asked tenderly, "What's the matter? You've been miss-
ing me a whole lot, huh?" And she, finally drying her eyes,
sniffed and nodded and bravely smiled and answered him
with the question, yes, weren't women silly?

Now record your thoughts and feelings about the story. Is there anything in
the story that reminds you of your own life or the life of someone you know?

A Closer Look

Reread the story more carefully. Then answer the following questions. In
what ways has your understanding of the story and its characters changed or
stayed the same after your more careful reading? Have any of your feelings
and opinions changed? Record this information on paper.

Sharing the Possibilities

When we share our responses to a story, we often discover that our ideas differ significantly. What might account for these differences in opinion? Half
the fun of reading literature is the sharing of ideas.

Dialogue Journal
A conventional journal typically contains the personal impressions of only
one reader. In addition, the traditional journal is usually shared with only the

teacher. A dialogue journal, on the other hand, is quite different. Two or more people record their thoughts in a dialogue journal. Together the writers explore their understanding of a literary work. Before talking face-to-face, they "talk" or dialogue on paper.

Choose a partner. Together you will create a dialogue journal by following the four steps below. Before you start, decide who will be Student A and who will be Student B.

Step One—For this activity, you will need five sheets of 8 1/2 by 11 inch paper. On each sheet draw two columns similar to the ones shown below. Label the left column "Student A" and the right column "Student B." Staple the five sheets of paper together at the upper left-hand corner.

Step Two—Student A should answer questions 1a through 5b before giving the dialogue journal to Student B. Student A must leave the right column blank for Student B's responses. See example below.

Student A Name	Student B Name Page 1

1. a. To me "grave sin of
      omission" means
 	
(Student A writes his or her answer here)
 	
  b. Esther reacts to the red-faced man by
 	
(Student A writes his or her answer here)
	(Leave blank for Student B)

Dialogue Journal, Page One
> 1. a. In paragraph 3, Esther is described as having committed a "grave sin of omission." *What does this phrase mean to you?*
>   b. *How does Esther react to the behavior of the red-faced man?* (Look only at paragraphs 6–14.)

Dialogue Journal, Page Two

2. a. In paragraphs 15–17, Esther's attitude toward the confrontation on the bus changes. *Where in these paragraphs do you first notice a change in her attitude?*

   b. Beginning with paragraph 16, Esther recalls painful memories of a streetcar ride that occurred many years ago. *Briefly describe these memories in your own words.*

Dialogue Journal, Page Three

3. a. *Why do you think Esther feels so angry about the "I AM _____" buttons in general? How does she feel toward the old man wearing the "I AM KOREAN" button?*

   b. As you read paragraphs 18–21, imagine the scene inside the bus.

   How does Esther try to communicate her thoughts to the "little woman"? Imagine for a moment that you are the "little woman." *What are you thinking as you look at Esther with a "face so impassive yet cold, and eyes so expressionless yet hostile"?*

Dialogue Journal, Page Four

4. a. Reread paragraphs 18–21. *If the "little woman" and Esther had spoken to each other, what do you think they would have said?*

   b. "There arose in [Esther's] mind some words . . . Do not regard what he says, now that he is in liquor. Perhaps it is the only time he ought to be regarded." *What do these sentences mean to you?*

Dialogue Journal, Page Five

5. a. In paragraph 23, Yamamoto writes that Esther was once again overwhelmed with the "sensation of there being in the world nothing solid." *At what other time in her life do you think Esther felt this helpless, sickening sensation? Why do you believe Esther feels this way now?*

   b. In paragraph 24, Esther chooses not to tell Buro about her experience. *Why do you think she does this?*

Step Three—Next, Student B should carefully read and respond to each of Student A's answers. Do you agree or disagree with Student A? What would you say if he or she were sitting next to you? Neatly write or type your responses in the right-hand column marked "Student B." See example on the following page.

Step Four—Finally, get together to talk over your answers and your journal experience.

Student A	Student B
Name	Name Page 1
1. a. To me "grave sin of omission" means *(Student A's answer)* b. Esther reacts to the red-faced man by *(Student A's answer)*	1. a. I disagree/agree with you because *(Student B responds to Student A here)* b. I think your description of Esther's reaction is good but you forgot to mention *(Student B responds to Student A here)*

Understanding Flashbacks

Plot refers to the pattern of events that takes place in a story. Most of the time, authors order events chronologically. That is, the story's action unfolds much like real life events do—the story imitates real time.

However, authors sometimes use a *flashback,* a device that interrupts the chronological sequence of events. When a character thinks, dreams, or talks about things that happened prior to the beginning of the story, he or she is said to have a flashback. These reveries provide important clues as to what motivates the character to behave in one way and not in another.

How can a reader recognize a flashback when it occurs? It's easy. A change in verb tense from simple past or past progressive to past perfect can signal a flashback. The author indicates the conclusion of the flashback by switching back to the simple past tense form.

In the following paragraph from "Doors," notice the switch in verb tense from simple past (the action as it occurs in the story) to the past perfect (the flashback or events that happened before the story began) and back to simple past again (action which resumes the story).

> Deepak *was puzzled* by all of this door-shutting. He himself *had grown up* in a large family, and although they *had been* affluent enough to possess three bedrooms, they *had* never *observed* boundaries. They *had* constantly *spilled* into each others' rooms. He *asked* Asha about it one day. She *wasn't* able to give him an answer.

This flashback gives the reader valuable insight into Deepak's character and why he is so impatient with his wife's obsession with doors.

Esther experiences just one significant flashback. Skim the story in order to locate it. Where does the tense change take place?

Extending the Reading Experience

Scenario

Look again at paragraphs 18–21. Imagine for a moment that you are the "little woman." What are you thinking as you look at Esther with a "face so impassive yet cold, and eyes so expressionless yet hostile"? If the woman and Esther had interacted, what would they have said to each other? What would they have done? With your dialogue journal partner, write a scene in which Esther and the "little woman" are interacting. (For ideas, use your answers to questions 3b and 4a in your dialogue journal.)

Focus on Language

Symbols

A symbol is a concrete image that represents an abstract idea. For instance, the sun is often used to represent life. Because symbols sometimes elicit

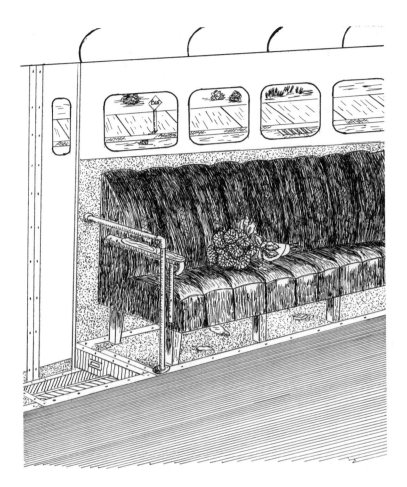

strong emotional responses from readers, fiction writers use them often to enrich readers' experience with a story and to broader their understanding of the work.

Sometimes, however, symbols conjure up different concepts for readers depending on the readers' cultural backgrounds. Even color can be symbolic, and it is often culture bound. For example, in mainstream America *black* has been traditionally linked to death and funerals, whereas in Korea *white* is the color for funerals.

In "Wilshire Bus," Yamamoto mentions one particular concrete image several times—the yellow and red chrysanthemums. Decide if you think these flowers and their colors have any symbolic, even cultural, significance in the story.

Consult the "Additional Works of Interest" section for a list of materials about Japanese-Americans.

UNIT 8

"Saturday Morning Memorial" by Mykel D. Myles

Meet the Author

Mykel D. Myles is an award-winning poet and short story writer, as well as an essayist. His first published poem was written when he was still a teenager. He was born and raised in Cleveland, Ohio, where he still resides and where he works as a journalist and editor in chief for a local newspaper. To his list of literary accomplishments, Myles has added a first novel, *The Long Night of the Demon.*

Preparing to Read

The Wisdom of Elders

In 1619, a Dutch ship set sail across the great Atlantic. Below deck lay twenty frightened Africans bound for Jamestown, Virginia, transported not as free men but as slaves. For more than two hundred years, slave ships continued to carry human cargo and suffering to North America. Conditions for slaves on board these ships were unimaginably bad. Hundreds of men, women, and children lay side by side, packed into the holds of the vessels, shackled and unable to move. Many died before ever reaching the shores of America. Those who did survive the passage were sold like cattle. Family members were often separated—husband from wife, parents from children. Such separations caused lifelong suffering.

Once on the plantations, keeping a family whole was of great importance to the slave. Consequently, the mere threat of resale (and decimation of family) was one of the most powerful mechanisms of control that the plantation owner had.

Slaves lived very hard lives, toiling long hours in fields and mansions. Nevertheless, African-Americans managed to survive more than two hundred years of slavery, thanks in great part to the family ties they struggled so hard to maintain. Integral to their kinship network were the elders, who served as storytellers and purveyors of folk wisdom, inspiring those younger, weaker, and less experienced than they to carry on in the face of unthinkable hardship.

Today many African-American elders, themselves descendants of slaves, continue to lend support to their families. They remain a vital influence in family and community life. In today's fast-paced world, the guidance of these elders is indispensable.

1. What roles have elders traditionally played in your culture?

   _____

2. How do elders in your country inspire, teach, and guide younger generations?

   _____

3. In what ways, if any, has their role *changed* in recent years?

   _____

4. What questions would you like to ask today's African-American elders, many of whom are descendants of slaves?

   _____

The First Reading

From the title of the poem, predict what you think the poem is about. Then read the poem, paying particular attention to the images described in the poem and to how you feel as you read. Remember to resist the temptation to reach for your dictionary.

Saturday Morning Memorial

Like Monarchs[1] gathering before
The last daisies of Autumn
We would come from all over town
To Momma's house on Saturday mornings
Whenever she called to say   5
"Uncle Benny's here"

---

1. Monarch—a type of butterfly

When you pulled into the drive
Before you even made it
Through the living room
              Through the music room   10
                   To the kitchen
Those still at home
Hurried the sleep from their eyes
And bounded down the stairs
To hear your "How ya doin', Squa-chee-wa!"[2]   15
And stand staring up in wondrous awe
At Grand-Uncle—so aged and stately
The doorway to our yesterdays
              The son of Tookie—Great Grand Mama
              Whose mother was Jenny the infant   20
              Carried in her mother's arms
              Through storm and darkest night
              Out of slavery
The past to us—so long ago
But alive in the blood and in the stories   25
So often told of how far we have come
And how far yet to go
You were our last man of olden days

And when we all arrived
Man! how the coffee flowed   30
Flavored with warmth and laughter
As we moved to the music room
Where Pine Top and Cow-Cow's
Boogie-Woogie[3] rang out
From the old upright[4]   35
That only you had mastered
And then the youngsters came
Fourth generation and fifth

---

2. Squa-chee-wa—Uncle Benny's pet name for his nephew Mykel Myles
3. Pine Top and Cow-Cow's Boogie-Woogie—Boogie-woogie is a form of American music
assumed to have originated in the rural South around the turn of the nineteenth century. It
reached its zenith in the mid- to late 1920s with the release of a song called "Cow-Cow's Boogie" by musician Cow-Cow Davenport. Then, in 1929, Clarence "Pine Top" Smith released a
tune called "Pine Top's Boogie-Woogie." Uncle Benny played blues piano and had a social and
working relationship with both Pine Top and Cow-Cow.
4. upright—a piano that sits "upright," unlike a grand piano. Therefore, it is called an *upright*
piano.

The windows of your tomorrows
To frolic around Uncle Benny   40
To feel your warming touch
Your kiss upon their cheeks
As you twisted your cap sidewise
And retold the stories
One more time   45

       2

How like you we have become
You who modeled for us
Manhood strong and tender
Who led us fatherless boys
Through the maze of adolescence   50
Coming by from way across town
To see us every week once or twice
To see how we were growing
        Thinking
            Learning   55
Speaking never of what we should do
But only of what you did
And how well it worked
Knowing or maybe only hoping
We would understand   60

Perhaps you knew how we loved you
How we admired you
How easily we would do it
Knowing that you had
I think you knew   65
Because of the way we would
Follow you out to your car
And your car down the drive
And wave as you sailed away
I think you knew well, Uncle   70
How much we loved you
        Learned from you
           Respected you
Such that even long after we entered manhood
When Uncle Benny came to visit   75
We still, fully grown

Gathered around you
   Brought your coffee mug
    Poured your "java"[5]
And sat to hear you   80
To look up to you
Still in wondrous awe
And listen

Fully grown men
Still coming to the fount   85
Of your infinitely good sense
Laughing with deeper voices now
And drinking our coffee, like you,
With more gusto
But still knowing the man among us   90
Still listening
   Learning
    Leaning
On the rod of your guidance
And still walking you to your car   95
   And down the drive
   And waving

    3

And even now on Saturday mornings
We sense your coming
Through the living room   100
   Where you feel the pictures
   Of our days together
Through the music room
   Where the piano stands
   Silent   105
To the kitchen
Where we sit at the table
Sipping our coffee
Reminiscing and laughing tenderly
As the sun beams down behind   110
The parting clouds
Reaching through the windows

---

5. java—coffee

To warmly touch our hands
And kiss our cheeks
As we fall silent   115
Thinking and leaning
On your legacy

Think back on "Saturday Morning Memorial."

1. What emotions did you feel as you moved through the poem?

_____

2. What memories does the poem stir in you?

_____

3. If you could meet Uncle Benny and his family, what questions would you ask them?

_____

4. What would you tell them about yourself and your own family?

_____

A Closer Look

Reread "Saturday Morning Memorial." Then write down your answers to the following questions on a separate sheet of paper.

1. What makes Uncle Benny so special?
2. Describe the family in the poem. What kind of relationship do the family members seem to have with each other?
3. What words and actions from the poem reflect their relationship? What parts of the poem do you find especially interesting or moving? Why do you suppose these parts have this effect on you?
4. Is any part of the poem confusing to you?
5. What do you like best about the poem?

Sharing the Possibilities

Imagine that you are a writer for a prominent literary magazine in your home country. Your editor has given you two assignments. Following the directions below, write two brief articles for your readers. At the top of each article, write your name and the title of your imaginary magazine. Be creative!

> Example: *Wei-hu Cheng, reviewer*
> *The Shanghai Journal of Literary Appreciation*

Interview with Uncle Benny
Your editor wants to include a human interest story—that is, an article about a fascinating person. Imagine that it is possible to meet Uncle Benny, talk to him, get to know him a bit. What does Uncle Benny look like in your imagination? How would you describe his disposition? Using the *poem* and your *imagination* as your guides, write an article describing Uncle Benny's personality and physical characteristics.

Second Impressions
Your second assignment is to write an article describing your impressions of "Saturday Morning Memorial." Begin by rereading the poem. Next look at your responses to "A Closer Look." Using them as your guide, write an article about your impressions of the poem. Important: Be sure to include the words and phrases from the poem that helped shape your ideas. Use quotation marks to indicate quoted (copied) material.

Share your literary impressions and your human interest story with your classmates. How do your impressions of the poem and your descriptions of Uncle Benny compare with those of your classmates? What do you suppose accounts for the differences and similarities?

A Compilation of Student Work

Create a class anthology of student articles. First, neatly recopy or type your literary impression and your human interest story, making revisions and corrections as necessary. Then divide the class into two teams (in the case of a large class, divide into four or more teams to create more than one anthology). One team should gather all of the students' articles and pictures together, put them into logical order, and then create a table of contents. The other team should design a cover that reflects the assignment and the class's individuality. (If your school has the resources, have a copy of the anthology made for each student.) Finally, securely bind the materials.

Understanding Imagery

Images

Reading a poem can be a sensuous, almost tactile experience. To help create this effect, the poet chooses words as carefully (or with as much abandon!) as a painter uses paint. A splash of color here, a flutter of movement there, a spattering of this, a dollop of that. A poem excites the senses and emotions of a reader, even before it arouses the intellect. These sensory details—the images—are at the heart of poetry.

Not all images are alike though. Some are *literal.* They describe a concrete or real scene as the lines below apparently do.

> Those still at home
> Hurried the sleep from their eyes
> And bounded down the stairs

In our mind's eye, we see children rubbing their sleepy eyes before they noisily scramble down the stairs to greet their favorite uncle.

Close your eyes and think of "Saturday Morning Memorial." Then describe the literal or concrete images (sights, sounds, tastes, even smells) that remain with you. Locate the words and phrases in the poem that trigger these images. Compare your images with a classmate's images.

Metaphor and Simile

While many images in poetry are literal, others are abstract or *figurative.*
With this type of image, the reader must change or extend the obvious meaning of the words. In the figurative image, the words do not represent merely a
real object or scene. Instead the figurative image has two jobs—to stimulate
the reader's senses (as the concrete image does) *and* to represent a concept, an
abstract idea. For instance, the image of a *stone wall* represents something
real and concrete—a barrier made of stone and mortar. Yet the wall may also
symbolize abstract concepts like *isolation* or *loneliness.*

Metaphor

Poets often compare two or more things that are essentially very different.
This comparison of two unlike things can stimulate the reader's imagination.
For example, the sentence "My horse is a pig" compares two very different
animals—a pig and a horse. How can a horse be a pig? The owner of the
horse is speaking *figuratively,* not literally. In using the comparison, the
speaker ascribes piglike *qualities* to his horse. Perhaps the horse eats too
much grain or enjoys (like pigs do) rolling in mud. Upon hearing this sentence, a listener might picture an overweight, mud-caked equine. This type of
comparison or analogy is called a *metaphor.* Poets frequently use metaphors.
For example, in "Saturday Morning Memorial," Mykel Myles compares
Uncle Benny to a doorway and his nephews to windows.

> And [we] stand staring up in wondrous awe
> At Grand-Uncle—so aged and stately
> The doorway to our yesterdays
>
> .   .   .   .
>
> And then the youngsters came
> Fourth generation and fifth
> The windows of your tomorrows

What do you make of these metaphors? Uncle Benny and his nephews are
human beings, yet doorways and windows are *objects.* How could Uncle
Benny be a doorway and his nephews be windows? Find these lines in the
poem. Working with a partner, extend the obvious or literal meanings of
doorway and *window.* Then finish the following sentences.

Uncle Benny is "the doorway to [his nephews'] yesterdays" because

_____.

The nephews are "the windows of [their uncle's] tomorrows" because

_____ .

Simile

Another type of analogy is the *simile*. Like metaphors, similes are figurative and they compare dissimilar things. Unlike metaphors though, similes use the words *like* and *as*. For example, the metaphor "My horse is a pig" becomes a simile with the simple addition of *like* or *as*—"My horse is *like* a pig" or "My horse is *as* sloppy *as* a pig." The effect is the same in all three sentences—the horse is given the characteristics of a pig.

Alone or with a partner, look closely at the following stanza taken from the poem.

> Like Monarchs gathering before
> The last daisies of Autumn
> We would come from all over town
> To Momma's house on Saturday mornings
> Whenever she called to say
> "Uncle Benny's here"

1. Does this stanza contain a simile, a metaphor, or both?

   _____

2. What (or who) is being compared to the monarchs?

   _____

3. What (or who) is being compared to the daisies?

   _____

Explain the analogies (comparisons) that you see in these lines.

Poetic Surprise

Poets often like to surprise their readers, to keep their readers slightly off balance. One way to do this is to place unusual ideas side by side. Look at the following lines from the poem.

> Man! how the coffee flowed
> Flavored with warmth and laughter

Being a liquid, coffee certainly "flows," and it can be flavored with sugar, cream, amaretto, even Irish whiskey. But coffee flavored with *warmth* and *laughter?* How could that be?

When you read these lines, what image does your mind's eye see? What mood do these lines create for you? Describe another time when coffee could be flavored this way. Could coffee be "flavored" in other ways?

Extending the Reading Experience

Do you have an "Uncle Benny" in your family—perhaps a grandfather, a grandmother, a granduncle, an aunt, even an older brother or sister? Why is this person special to you? What pet names did he or she use for you? What words of encouragement did this person give? In what ways is this special person *similar* to Uncle Benny in the poem? How is this person *different* from Uncle Benny? Describe this person to a classmate.

Create a written tribute to your special relative by doing the following.

1. In his poem, Mykel Myles recalls the many Saturday mornings he spent with his uncle Benny. He describes his excitement and anticipation, the mood of the visits, the details of his childhood home. Think back to the times you spent with your favorite older relative. Focus on an activity or event shared with this relative (perhaps Sunday afternoons in the park, a fishing trip, visits to the library). Mykel Myles learned about his ancestors from Uncle Benny. From his uncle's example he learned how to be a man. Did you learn any important lessons from your special relative? Write a narrative describing how you felt and what you did. Create a mood by using concrete images.
2. Try changing your story into a poem. You may want to use "Saturday Morning Memorial" as a model.
3. With your classmates, gather the class's poems and descriptions into a booklet by first neatly recopying each page and making revisions and corrections as necessary. Then design an attractive cover and a table of contents. Finally, secure the pages together.

Focus on Language

Denotation vs. Connotation

Many words have two types of meanings—denotation and connotation. The *denotative* meaning of a word is its *exact* or *literal* definition. It is devoid of emotional or cultural association. Take for instance the word *skull. Webster's New Collegiate Dictionary* defines this word as "the skeleton of the head of a vertebrate forming a bony or cartilaginous case that encloses and protects the brain and chief sense organs and supports the jaws." These are the words of the scientist—exact and literal. Unlike the denotative definition of a word, the *connotative* meaning has strong *emotional* and/or *cultural* implications. The word *skull* (along with the image that it conjures in the mind) is most often associated with *fear, death,* or *danger* and *feelings of uneasiness.* Literary artists take full advantage of such deep-seated emotional meanings attached to words.

Negative and Positive Connotations

Many words share similar denotative meanings, but their connotative meanings can be very different. For example, all of the following adjectives are synonyms since they share a common denotative meaning—they all mean "having less than the usual amount of fat."

skinny   thin   lean   slim   slender

Yet these words differ in their connotations. Three of the words—*slender, slim,* and *lean*—have positive connotations in American culture while relatively speaking the adjectives *skinny* and *thin* can have negative connotations since they suggest weakness.

The following verbs were taken from the poem. Match each verb in column A with *two* synonyms from column B by writing the letters of the correct items on the lines in column A. The first one is done for you.

Column A
1. _c, e_ The coffee was *flavored* with warmth and laughter.
2. ____ We *sipped* our coffee.
3. ____ The singer's voice *rang out* from the radio.
4. ____ The people *gathered* around the president.

Column B
a. blared
b. slurped
c. seasoned
d. swarmed
e. peppered
f. sampled
g. assembled
h. resonated

As we saw with the synonyms *skinny, thin, lean, slim,* and *slender,* synonyms may have different connotations. In other words, *synonyms* are not exactly the same in meaning but merely *similar* in meaning.

Using a dictionary, decide which verbs in columns A and B have negative connotations and which have positive connotations. Write the verbs in the correct columns below. The first one is done for you.

Verbs with Positive Connotations   Verbs with Negative Connotations

1. flavored, seasoned   peppered

2. _____   _____

3. _____   _____

4. _____   _____

See the "Additional Works of Interest" section for a list of books, sound recordings, and videos about African-American culture.

UNIT 9

"Thomas Iron-Eyes" by Marnie Walsh

Meet the Author

Born in 1916 in Sturgis, South Dakota, Marnie Walsh spent her childhood enjoying the beauty of the Black Hills region. She earned her B.A. from the Pennsylvania State University and her M.A. in creative writing from the University of New Mexico. Poetry from her book *A Taste of the Knife* is included in the Pushcart Press *Best of the Small Presses* anthology. Walsh was an accomplished writer and sportswoman and an advocate for Native American cultures. After raising a family of five sons and two daughters, Walsh and her husband, Mark, spent their later retirement years in Green Valley, Arizona, where on November 8, 1996, Marnie died at the age of seventy-nine.

Preparing to Read

The Native American

The original inhabitants of America were the American Indians, also known as Native Americans. The first Europeans arrived in America in the fifteenth century. Before their arrival, Native Americans lived a life free from European influence and domination. Because Native Americans could so ably adapt to their environment, they inhabited almost every area in North America. Eventually though, more and more Europeans came to America and claimed the land for themselves. As a result, the Indians were forced to leave the eastern part of the United States and move westward toward the Mississippi River and beyond. Increasingly, America became the province of European settlers. By the end of the nineteenth century, the U.S. government had claimed most of the land as its own. Government officials wanted to control the Indians, so they moved them onto special tracts of land called reservations. Here the Native Americans could not easily practice their customs. After they lost their freedom, American Indians were in danger of losing their culture as well.

Indian tribal areas of North America, 1580–1880 A.D. The dotted lines
reflect the present national, state, and provincial boundaries.

Think of another example of one culture dominating another. This can
be an example from your country's history or some other country's. What
were the names of the two cultures? (e.g., European and Native American)
How were the lives of the people changed by the domination?

_____

_____

The First Reading

As you read, do not concern yourself with every detail. Instead decide what
the general idea is.

Thomas Iron-Eyes
Born Circa 1840, Died 1919
Rosebud Agency
South Dakota

1

I woke before the day, when the night bird
Knocked three times upon my door
To warn the Other Sleep was coming.
By candlelight I painted the broad stripes
Of white across my forehead, the three scarlet spots   5
Upon my cheek. I greased well my braids
With sour fat from the cooking pan, then tied them
With a bit of string
Saved for this occasion.
From the trunk I took the dress of ceremony: 10
The breechclout and the elkskin shirt,
The smoke of their breath strong in my nose;
The smoke not of this time, this life or place
But of my youth, of many lodges I dwelt within,[1]
The pony raids, the counting coup.   15
The chase and kill of buffalo;
The smell of grass when it was green.
The smell of coming snows
When food was plentiful within the camp
And ice crept over the rivers.   20
I put on the dress: then the leggings with scalps,
Now thin and colorless as the hair
Of sickly animals, sinew tied along the seams;
And on my feet the red-beaded moccasins
Worn by none but the bravest of warriors   25
I lie here, my dry bones and ancient skin
Holding my old heart.
The day star finds me ready for the journey.

2

Another time, another life, another place,
My people would have wrapped me   30
In deerskin, sewed me in the finest hides:

---

1. lodges I dwelt within—houses that I lived in

Borne me in honor to the cottonwood bier,
Laying at my right hand the sacred pipe
And at my left the arrows and bow, the lance
I bound with thongs and hung   35
With the feathers from the eagle's breast.
Below the scaffold of the dead
My pony of the speckled[2] skin and fierce heart
Would be led, and with a blow[3] of the stone axe
Lie down to wait my needs.   40
Far above in the sacred hoop of the sky
Long-sighted hawks hanging on silent wings
Would mark my passing.

3

When the Life-Giver hid from the night
The dark wind would speak to my spirit   45
And I would arise, taking up my weapons.
Mounting my horse I would follow
The great path over the earth, beyond the stars.
I would see the glow of cooking fires
as bright as arrow tips across the northern sky;   50
Waiting for me, old friends would dance and feast
And play the games of gambling.
Behind me drums would beat and willow whistles cry
Like the doves of spring who nested
In the berry bushes near the river of my village.   55
I would pause to hear my sons in council,
Speaking of my deeds in war, my strength and wisdom.
My woman in her sorrow would tear her clothing,
Bloody her face marked with ashes,
And with a knife cut off her plaited[4] hair.   60

4

But I am Thomas, here, where no grass grows,
Where no clear rivers run;
Where dirt and despair abound,
Where heat and rain alike rust out

---

2. speckled—covered with spots
3. blow—a hit, as on the head
4. plaited—braided

The souls of my people, the roofs of tin;　　　　　65
Where disease like a serpent[5] slips from house to house
And hunger sits in the dooryard.
I am Thomas. I wait for the wagon
To bring the government box of pine;
I wait for the journey to the burying ground　　　　　70
Below the sandy butte[6] where rattlesnakes
Stink in burrows, and the white man's wooden trinities[7]
Stand in crooked rows.
There I will be put beneath the earth.
They will seal in my spirit.　　　　　75
I will not hear the dark wind's cry
To come and take the starry road
Across the circle of the sky.

In your opinion, what is the main idea of "Thomas Iron-Eyes"? List some of the words and phrases that helped you decide.

_____

_____

_____

_____

5. serpent—snake
6. butte—a small mountain with steep sides
7. trinities—crucifixes

A Closer Look

In the following activity, you will research and then present information about the Plains Indians of North America. This activity will increase your understanding of "Thomas Iron-Eyes" and the world of the Native American.

Doing Research
Divide into groups of four or five researchers. Each research group should choose one of the four general topics listed below. Under each are vocabulary words taken from the poem. Work together to find information about the general topic and the vocabulary words. To find information, visit your school's library as well as the public library. (Some universities and communities have special organizations devoted to preserving the cultures of indigenous people.) Gather information from a variety of resources such as textbooks, reference books, videos, and if possible, the Internet. (For a list of resources, consult the "Additional Works of Interest" section in this book. A reference librarian can suggest other resources.) Keep a special folder used exclusively for your research materials such as notes and pictures. What can your group do to ensure the gathering of sufficient and accurate information?

General Topic 1: Clothing/Appearance of the Plains Indians

Clothing	Materials	Physical Appearance
breechcloth (clout)	deerskin	braids
(beaded) moccasins	elkskin	
leggings		

General Topic 2: Hunting Practices of the Plains Indians

Animals	Weapons	Tools
buffalo	bow	stone ax (axe)
elk	arrow	
deer	lance	

General Topic 3: War Customs of the Plains Indians

counting coup	scalps
warrior	pony raids

General Topic 4: Death Rituals of the Plains Indians

bier	scaffold for the dead	sacred pipe

Presenting the Information

Once your group has completed its research, decide on the best way to present the information to the rest of the class. Your group should consider the following questions. What information should we share? What will we say? Will we use notes or an outline as we speak? Who will talk first, second, third, and so on? How will our group capture the audience's interest? Will our group use audiovisual aids such as pictures, posters, video and audio recordings, charts, and maps? What equipment will we need? When and where should the group rehearse? What else can our group do to ensure a smooth and interesting presentation?

Sharing the Possibilities

The following activity will help you explore the poem more deeply. For this activity, the poem has been divided into six sections. Read each part on your own, then respond to the questions that follow. Write your answers in a chart like the one shown. Divide notebook paper in half to form two columns. Write in the headings and the questions, leaving space for your answers. Periodically review your responses to the questions and change them if necessary. Later share your charts with a classmate. Explain to your partner how you arrived at your answers. Remember that you and your partner can disagree. As you work with your partner, use the poem to help support your answers.

My Responses to Questions for Section One	My Thoughts and Feelings about Section One
1. a. Describe what you think is happening in section one. b. What do you think is the "Other Sleep"? c. What could "this occasion" be?	

Thomas Iron-Eyes
Born Circa 1840, Died 1919
Rosebud Agency
South Dakota

Section 1

I woke before the day, when the night bird
Knocked three times upon my door
To warn the Other Sleep was coming.
By candlelight I painted the broad stripes
Of white across my forehead, the three scarlet spots   5
Upon my cheek. I greased well my braids
With sour fat from the cooking pan, then tied them
With a bit of string
Saved for this occasion.

1. a. Describe what you think is happening in this section of the poem.
   b. What do you think the "Other Sleep" is?
   c. What could "this occasion" in the last line be?

Now explain your answers to your partner.

Section 2

From the trunk I took the dress of ceremony: 10
The breechclout and the elkskin shirt,
The smoke of their breath strong in my nose;
The smoke not of this time, this life or place
But of my youth, of many lodges I dwelt within,
The pony raids, the counting coup.   15
The chase and kill of buffalo;
The smell of grass when it was green.
The smell of coming snows
When food was plentiful within the camp
And ice crept over the rivers.   20

2. a. Is the narrator of the poem young or old? How do you know this?
   b. What does the narrator seem to be describing in this section?
   c. What questions does this section raise in your mind?

Now share your answers with your partner. Don't forget to explain how you arrived at your answers.

Section 3

I put on the dress: then the leggings with scalps,
Now thin and colorless as the hair
Of sickly animals, sinew tied along the seams;
And on my feet the red-beaded moccasins
Worn by none but the bravest of warriors   25
I lie here, my dry bones and ancient skin
Holding my old heart.
The day star finds me ready for the journey.

3. a. The narrator seems to be preparing for something unusual to hap-
       pen. What do you think that could be? What words in the text
       make you say this?
   b. Can you make any guesses about what is to come? For instance, the
       narrator says he or she is ready for a journey, but a journey to
       where?

Now explain your answers to your partner.

Section 4

Another time, another life, another place,
My people would have wrapped me   30
In deerskin, sewed me in the finest hides:
Borne me in honor to the cottonwood bier,
Laying at my right hand the sacred pipe
And at my left the arrows and bow, the lance
I bound with thongs and hung   35
With the feathers from the eagle's breast.
Below the scaffold of the dead
My pony of the speckled skin and fierce heart
Would be led, and with a blow of the stone axe
Lie down to wait my needs.   40
Far above in the sacred hoop of the sky
Long-sighted hawks hanging on silent wings
Would mark my passing.

4. a. Describe what the first line means to you—"Another time, another life, another place."
   b. How would you describe the narrator's attitude toward the other time, life, and place?
   c. What words in the poem reveal his attitude?

How do your answers compare to your partner's?

Section 5

When the Life-Giver hid from the night
The dark wind would speak to my spirit   45
And I would arise, taking up my weapons.
Mounting my horse I would follow
The great path over the earth, beyond the stars.
I would see the glow of cooking fires
as bright as arrow tips across the northern sky;   50
Waiting for me, old friends would dance and feast
And play the games of gambling.
Behind me drums would beat and willow whistles cry
Like the doves of spring who nested
In the berry bushes near the river of my village.   55
I would pause to hear my sons in council,
Speaking of my deeds in war, my strength and wisdom.

My woman in her sorrow would tear her clothing,
Bloody her face marked with ashes,
And with a knife cut off her plaited hair.   60

5. a. What is the place or experience described in this section?
   b. What emotions does the narrator appear to be feeling as he tells of
      this place or experience?

Share your responses with your partner. Do you agree or disagree?

Section 6

But I am Thomas, here, where no grass grows,
Where no clear rivers run;
Where dirt and despair abound,
Where heat and rain alike rust out
The souls of my people, the roofs of tin;   65
Where disease like a serpent slips from house to house
And hunger sits in the dooryard.
I am Thomas. I wait for the wagon
To bring the government box of pine;
I wait for the journey to the burying ground   70
Below the sandy butte where rattlesnakes
Stink in burrows, and the white man's wooden trinities
Stand in crooked rows.
There I will be put beneath the earth.
They will seal in my spirit.   75
I will not hear the dark wind's cry
To come and take the starry road
Across the circle of the sky.

6. a. What emotions does the narrator seem to be feeling in this section
      of the poem? Why do you suppose he feels this way?
   b. Describe the emotions you feel as you read this section of the
      poem.
   c. Why do you think the narrator waited until this point in the poem
      to refer to himself as "Thomas"?
   d. Describe the mood of this section compared to the mood of the
      rest of the poem.

Now share your answers to part six with your partner. Don't forget to explain how you arrived at your answers.

Now listen as your teacher reads the poem from the beginning. Then describe the images that came to your mind as you heard the poem. Describe the emotions that you felt.

Understanding Simile

Poets often employ *similes,* the comparison of two or more things that are essentially quite different. This comparison of two unlike things provokes the reader's imagination and increases his or her emotional response to a poem or story. For example, "Vladimir eats like a bird" compares two very different creatures—a human and a bird. But the comparison lets us know that Vladimir has a small or birdlike appetite. We might imagine him to be a delicate, even weak, individual. With the use of the word *like,* such a comparison is called a simile.

Doing the following activity will help you better understand similes.

1. Disease like a serpent slips from house to house

   In this line, disease is compared to a serpent. How are disease and a serpent similar?

   _____

   How are they different?

   _____

   Write a paragraph describing how you feel when you read that disease is "like a serpent" slipping from house to house.

2. Behind me drums would beat and willow whistles cry
   Like the doves of spring who nested

   In the lines above what two things are being compared?

   _____

   How are these two things similar? _____

   How are they different? _____

3. I would see the glow of cooking fires
   As bright as arrow tips across the northern sky

In these lines, the glow of cooking fires is being compared to arrow tips. In what ways are cooking fires and arrow tips similar?

_____

How are they different?

_____

4. Look again at the similes in 1, 2, and 3 to find the two words commonly used to introduce similes.

Extending the Reading Experience

Imaginary Video Production

What would the poem "Thomas Iron-Eyes" look like if it were made into a movie? What special concerns would a director or a stage designer have? This activity lets you explore the possibility of making a video. Don't worry though. This will be an imaginary video production. You won't need a video camera—just a lot of imagination.

Divide into groups of three or four students. Each group or production team will decide how the poem would look and sound if it were made into a movie. Team members will decide on scenery, props, make–up, and special effects, among other things. Once your team is assembled, do the following.

1. Give your team a special name. For instance, Fantastico Images, Inc.
2. Complete each of the five tasks below.
   Important: Be sure to use the words in the poem and your imagination as your guides. Take copious notes as you work with your team. You will use these notes to write paragraphs.

Task 1. Using your notes, write a paragraph or "script" describing in detail how your team would portray Thomas Iron-Eyes. Use the information below as a guide.

> Thomas Iron-Eyes
> Based on the poem's description of Thomas, decide how best to bring him to life. Ask yourself: How does Thomas look, act, and move in the poem? How do his tone of voice, his actions, and his appearance change as he "moves" from stanza to stanza? What costumes, makeup, and gestures would best portray these changes? What other concerns should the team have?

Task 2. Using your notes, write a paragraph or "script" describing in detail what special effects your team would use. Use the information below as a guide.

> Special Effects
> Based on the team members' interpretations of the poem, decide on the special effects—lighting, music, natural sounds—that would bring the poem to life. Ask yourself: At what points in the poem should music begin and end? What parts of the poem call for silence, natural sounds, a drastic change in volume or type of music? Is there music from my native culture that would be suitable; if so, where in the poem should it be played? What parts of the poem demand bright lighting, dim lighting, darkness? Are there parts of the poem that call for different colors of lights? What colors and where and why one color and not another?

Task 3. Using your notes, write a paragraph or "script" describing in detail how your team would use props. Use the following information as a guide.

> Props
> Based on the poem's descriptions of Thomas's life, consider which props to use. Ask yourself: Which are the most important objects in the poem to be portrayed? What makes one object more important than another? And how would the props be used, either by Thomas himself or as part of the scenery?

Task 4. Using your notes, write a paragraph or "script" describing in detail how your team would portray the setting. Use the following information as a guide.

> Setting
> Based on your interpretations of the poem, decide how your team would portray the setting. Ask yourself: Should the poem be staged indoors or outdoors or using a combination of both? How could you best represent such things as the sandy butte or the rattlesnake burrows? What else should be considered for the setting?

Task 5. Using your notes, write a paragraph or "script" describing in detail how your team would portray minor characters. Use the information below as a guide.

Minor Characters
Based on your interpretations of the poem, decide how best to portray the poem's minor characters. Ask yourself: How should Thomas's wife, sons, and old friends be portrayed? Should they be seen or just heard? And how would you portray such "characters" as hunger sitting in the dooryard?

Final Draft of the "Scripts"
Gather your team's "scripts" into one booklet. Neatly recopy each page, making revisions and corrections as necessary. Design an attractive cover that captures your team's individuality. An optional table of contents can be useful for readers. Finally, securely bind the pages together.

Final Step of the "Production"
Your production team should now meet to discuss the overall effectiveness of its "production." To do this, examine your team's final draft. With your team, discuss the following questions. How well did our team capture the spirit of the poem? What could we have done better? Would our team's video production excite the audience? How would the audience feel as they left the theater? What questions would we want the audience members to ask themselves as they drove home? How could our group have worked better together?

Individual Activity
On your own, write an essay explaining in detail how well you think your team captured the spirit of the poem. Conclude by exploring what your group could have done better.

Focus on Language

Shifts in Tense

Authors can use verb tense to show elaborate shifts in time and perspective. Marnie Walsh, author of "Thomas Iron-Eyes," uses multiple shifts in time and perspective to reveal the course of Thomas's life. The following activity will help you to better understand Thomas's complex life.

Time and Perspective Analysis
Divide into groups of three or four students. Some groups should work on
stanzas one and four, while others work on stanzas two and three. Each
group should prepare a time line on paper. Make yours large enough to
accommodate Thomas's actions. Follow the directions below.

Stanzas One and Four
If your group was assigned stanzas one and four, locate the main verbs in
these stanzas. Next indicate approximately where Thomas's actions fall on
the group's time line. What verb tenses occur in stanzas one and four?
Finally, share your group's time line with another group assigned to do stanzas one and four. How do the time lines compare?

Stanzas Two and Three
If your group was assigned stanzas two and three, locate the main verbs in
these stanzas. Next indicate approximately where Thomas's actions fall on

the group's time line. What modal is used repeatedly in stanzas two and three? What is the meaning of this modal? Look at the first line of stanza two. How does this line help you understand the actions in stanzas two and three? Finally, share your group's time line with another group assigned to do the same stanzas. How do the time lines compare?

All Stanzas

If your group looked at stanzas one and four, meet with a group who looked at stanzas two and three. Compare time lines. What do your combined time lines say about Thomas's passage through time? Explain how your time lines reveal shifts in time and perspective.

See the "Additional Works of Interest" section for a list of books, sound recordings, and videos about Native American cultures.

Notes for Teachers

Unit 1. "Doors" by Chitra Divakaruni

Focus on Language

Sample Answers
1. Deepak and his family had moved freely (like water) into each others' rooms because the doors were always open.
2. Asha couldn't move as Raj's rhythmic voice disappeared beyond the bend of the stairs.
3. Asha could easily hear Raj's eager voice. The bedroom door could not shut his voice out.
4. The coldness and darkness of the night slowly surrounded Asha. She felt alone in her room.

Unit 2. "Farewell" by Liz Sohappy Bahe

Focus on Language

Below is a framework for the repetitions found in "Farewell."

You _____.
I _____ not _____
but _____.
You _____.
I _____ not _____
but _____.
You _____.
I _____ not _____
but _____.
You _____.
I _____.

Additional Activity—Focus on Negation
If students have questions about the unusual use of negation in the poem, the teacher can use the following minilesson. Italicized sentences should be written on the board or overhead.

121

I watched not the tools or chips fly.

Above is a line from the poem "Farewell." Notice how the negative adverb *not* follows the main verb. In English, *not* follows only modals: "I will (do/can/must/ought/etc.) not . . ." The word *not* does not normally follow the main verb of the sentence as it does in this poem. In standard modern English, this sentence would read "I did not watch the tools or chips fly." Compare the word order of the two sentences below.

a. *I watched not the tools or chips fly.*
b. *I did not watch the tools or chips fly.*

Why do you think Bahe placed *not* after the main verb in the poem?
How does the rhythm of sentence a compare to that of sentence b? Which sentence pattern do you prefer for the poem? Why?
Change the following sentences from "Farewell" so that the word *not* is in its usual place. Make other necessary changes.

1. *I danced not to thundering drums.*
2. *I went there not to meet your people.*

Unit 3. "La Puerta" by José Antonio Burciaga

Extending the Reading Experience

C. *Lotería Nacional*—A Scenario
This scenario is worth doing for it can have unexpected and fun results. Each actor for this scenario will *not* know in advance what the other will do or say. This way, the actors respond to each other much as they would in real life, for in reality, we cannot read other people's thoughts or know in advance what they are going to say or do. As Robert DiPietro says (DiPietro 1987)

Participants in a well-founded scenario soon discover that they cannot simply play out prescribed roles. They cannot take for granted that they will achieve their goals simply by acting out conventional or stock lines supplied by the text or the teacher. . . . The variables affecting the performance of the students playing A and B are too numerous for the teacher to control or even anticipate. These variables include the students' state of preparedness, how they happen to feel that day, certainly how they will react to each other once they begin to perform. Such matters should not concern the teacher. It is soon apparent that the same scenario will never be acted out in identical ways twice in a row. This variability is the strength of the scenario as a pedagogical device. It enables learners to fit the target language to their own preferences. (49–50)

The class can be divided into two groups (or four groups, depending on the size of the class—four groups would result in two very different enactments of the same scenario). Group members should be instructed to work together to devise a plan of action for their particular character. Each group is to keep its strategies a secret from the other groups. The most that they can know is the identity of the other character. After each group creates a plan of action for its character, it should choose a person to act out the scene.

Students should be told that the key to creating a plan of action is to map out several ways to deal with the situation. This requires them to try to anticipate the behavior of the other character. Of course, students will not be able to predict exactly what will happen or what the other character will do or say, nor should they be able to. The advantage of the scenario is that as it is "performed" the action unfolds naturally and according to each player's (actor's) own judgments about the other's motives.

The teacher should answer any questions about vocabulary but keep directing of the students' planning to a bare minimum. The students should be given approximately fifteen minutes to plan their strategies.

Unit 6. "The Purchase" by Nick C. Vaca

Focus on Language

Sample Answers

1. The young man knew it was morally and legally wrong to *steal* something from his neighbor.
2. Louis wasn't sure how to act around girls since he *had just left (had just graduated from)* an all-boys school.
3. Can you go to the store? We *do not have any* milk.
4. I *am very clumsy on my feet. I am very clumsy with my hands.*
5. He *barely passed* Calculus I.
6. Are you sure he's not *telling you a lie?*
7. *Hurry up!*
8. Let's *be friends again.*
9. You're *fooling me.* I was sure he'd *fail* the class.
10. He always *tries very hard* to help his students learn physics.
11. When I came home three hours past my curfew, my dad *became very angry.* He told me either *improve my behavior or move out.*
12. I don't know what's *bothering* my brother. He must *be in a bad mood* this morning.
13. She just bought a new car. Normally it's very expensive, but the dealer is going out of business, so she *bought it for very little money.*
14. I think maybe you've *decided to do more than you can realistically accomplish.* Don't you think you might be *getting involved in too many activities? Don't underestimate my abilities.*

Unit 7. "Wilshire Bus" by Hisaye Yamamoto

Preparing to Read

Additional Background Information

Hisaye Yamamoto and her family spent a number of years in one of ten relocation camps set aside for Japanese-Americans during World War II. The following is additional background information that may help students better understand the context of "Wilshire Bus" and the nature of the times. What follows is by no means an exhaustive account but merely a modest overview. It augments information found in "Preparing to Read." The source for the following overview is Page Smith's *Democracy on Trial: The Japanese-American Evacuation and Relocation in World War II* (New York: Simon and Schuster, 1995). There are dozens of other excellent books that describe this tragic history in detail. See the bibliography and the "Additional Works of Interest" section for additional resources.

Like most immigrants to the United States in the nineteenth and early twentieth centuries, the initial wave of Japanese immigrants left their homeland for economic reasons. Desperate poverty drove them from Japan, while the promise of jobs drew them to America's shores. At the same time, it was not unusual for the Issei (first-generation immigrants) to plan to return to their homeland after they had worked for several years diligently saving money for a better life upon their return. Indeed some 20,000 Japanese remigrated home by the late 1930s. Such a desire to return home after a sojourn in the United States was not unique to the Japanese. Millions of Poles, Croatians, Serbs, Slavs, and Slovaks returned to Eastern Europe after a few years. Of the roughly 4,300,000 immigrants who came to the United States at that time, 1,452,239 eventually found their way home.

Many of the immigrants who had every intention of leaving the United States one day held fast to old ways and refused to learn English or assimilate into the American culture. In contrast, other Japanese found the United States to their liking and decided to stay, learning English and adopting American ways, even taking English first names. At the same time though, many Nisei (second-generation Japanese-Americans) held both U.S. and Japanese citizenship, and after 1924, children born to Japanese living in the United States could be made citizens of Japan, even though they were born in the United States. Many of these children were sent either to Japan for a Japanese education or to Japanese government–sponsored language schools in the United States (by 1940, there were 261 such schools in California alone). For many Issei, such education was primarily an attempt to hold on to their "Japanese-ness," while for some it was a show of devotion to the Japanese emperor and nationalism. (It is very important to point out that the Issei were denied U.S. citizenship by the U.S. government. This may in part explain their deep devotion to Japan.) Many Americans not of Japanese descent were uneasy with these educational arrangements and perceived the dual citizenship as a dangerous division of loyalty.

Despite the wariness, relations between the two groups remained relatively stable, that is, until the morning of December 7, 1941, when everything changed. On this date the Japanese air force bombed Pearl Harbor, an American naval base in the Pacific, killing and wounding thousands of military personnel and civilians alike. The immediate response to the attack was shock and an increase in hostility toward Japanese-Americans on the West Coast. It is important to point out here though that many individuals and organizations came to the defense of Japanese-Americans. Nevertheless, suspicion, fear, and racism prevailed and led to tragic results for the Japanese living in the United States. One consequence of the attack on Pearl Harbor was a deep division among the West Coast Japanese themselves. Three groups formed—the Issei, whose loyalties for the most part lay with Japan; the Nisei who had been educated in the principles of unquestioning devotion to the emperor; and the Americanized Nisei, most of whom had attended American high school and often a college or university and who openly declared their loyalty to the United States. On March 2, 1942, General John Dewitt ordered the "voluntary" evacuation of "all persons of Japanese ancestry." Soon afterward the order was changed from voluntary to "controlled" or *mass* evacuation to relocation camps. During the spring and summer of 1942, some 110,000 men, women, and children of Japanese ancestry were forced to leave their homes and businesses and enter ten relocation centers. They lost their homes, businesses, and personal property. Rather than sell their possessions (many of which were priceless antiques) or leave them for looters, many Japanese-Americans destroyed them. The tens of thousands of Japanese who had worked decades to build businesses and acquire homes saw their houses and stores overrun by vulturelike junk sellers and used-furniture dealers. Despite such harsh treatment, nearly 26,000 Japanese-Americans served in the U.S armed forces during World War II. Many were cited for bravery.

For four decades, the shameful reality of the relocation camps remained largely hidden from the American public. It wasn't until 1988 that the U.S. government offered an apology for the mistreatment and paid partial restitution to the approximately 60,000 surviving Japanese-Americans who had been confined.

Extending the Reading Experience

Additional Activity—A Scenario
This is an additional activity the teacher may wish to try with more advanced groups. Refer to the scenario directions in Unit 3 in the Notes for Teachers.

Each group should be given a copy of one of the roles below.

Role (Student A)

> You are the driver of the bus in which Esther is riding. Your boss recently warned you to keep things under control on the bus. You notice that the red-faced man is causing trouble. However, you are almost certain that he is a personal friend of the owner of the bus company. Prepare yourself to deal with the man.

Role (Student B)

> You are the red-faced man. You never drink. But you do have a serious medical
> condition that sometimes makes you look and act like you are drunk. This has
> caused you problems in the past. However, you want to keep this medical condi-
> tion a secret. Prepare yourself for an encounter with the bus driver.

After the groups have prepared their actors' plans of action, the actors should then
interact using the strategies that their respective groups have devised to guide them.
Instruct the actors to allow the scenario to unfold naturally as it would in real life.
After about ten minutes of interaction, the class should discuss its reactions to the
scenario.

Unit 8. "Saturday Morning Memorial" by Mykel D. Myles

Preparing to Read

Additional Background Information
Below is an expanded version of material found under "Preparing to Read." Students should be encouraged to read this information and to see the bibliography and
the "Additional Works of Interest" section for more resources on African-American
history and the slave trade.

Portugal and Spain authorized slave trade to the Americas in the early 1500s.
Trade continued in the Spanish colonies until 1880. In 1619, a Dutch ship set sail
across the great Atlantic. Below deck lay twenty frightened Africans bound for
Jamestown, Virginia, transported not as free men but as slaves. When the ship landed
at Jamestown, the captain delivered the slaves as promised in exchange for food. For
more than two hundred years, slave ships continued to carry human cargo to North
America. On the eve of the American Revolution, as many as 150,000 slaves lived in
Virginia alone. According to Philip D. Curtin, author of *The Atlantic Slave Trade: A
Census* (Madison: University of Wisconsin Press, 1969), total *imports* of slaves to
British America for the entire period of trade amounted to 2,064,000. For the same
period, the total number of *imports* for *all the Americas* came to 9,566,000.

A few early measures were taken to prohibit slavery in colonial America. The
Vermont Constitution of 1777 was the first document to abolish slavery. On March
2, 1807, Congress forbade trading in slaves with Africa. Nevertheless, *owning* slaves
continued to be legal throughout most of the United States until the middle of the
nineteenth century.

Conditions for slaves on board ships were unimaginably bad. Hundreds of men,
women, and children lay side by side, packed into the holds of the vessels, shackled
and unable to move. This method of transport was known as "tight-packing," done
so that more slaves could be carried per passage to the New World. Such overcrowd-
ing encouraged the spread of disease. Many slaves died before ever reaching America. (In an effort to keep more slaves alive, some captains used an alternative method
of transport known as "loose-packing." As the term implies, fewer slaves were

crammed into the hold. "Loose-packing" was not employed as often as "tight-packing," presumably, because the latter was more "economical.") Those who did survive the voyage were sold at auction like cattle. Family members were often separated—husband from wife, parents from children—at auction or subsequently on the plantation. In fact, the threat of sale (and separation of family) was always the most powerful mechanism of control that the plantation owner wielded.

Slaves lived very hard lives, toiling long hours in the fields and mansions. They suffered unspeakable cruelties and humiliation at the hands of slaveholders. They were forbidden to learn to read or write and even to speak their native languages and practice their customs. Despite these hardships, African-Americans managed not only to survive but to flourish, contributing significantly to American culture. A major reason for their survival was the "strength of family ties in a wide, extended-family kinship network characteristic of both North American black and African culture" (Harris 1992, 149), as well as the African tradition of holding the village elders in high regard. Elders, admired for their wisdom, have long served as story-tellers and purveyors of knowledge, giving guidance to those younger and less experienced. It was this deep-seated need for kinship and the respect for elders that helped hold the African-American family together. Today many African-American elders, descendants of the slaves of old, continue to lend support to their families. They remain vital to the stability of family and community life. In today's fast-paced world, the guidance of these elders is indispensable.

Following is an expanded version of the footnote explaining Pine Top and Cow-Cow's Boogie-Woogie that appears with "Saturday Morning Memorial." The information was supplied by the poem's author, Mykel Myles.

Boogie-woogie is a form of American music assumed to have originated in the rural South around the turn of the nineteenth century, more or less simultaneously with the blues. But the style owes more to ragtime than to the blues. It reached its zenith in the mid- to late 1920s with the release of a song called "Cow-Cow's Boogie" by musician Cow-Cow Davenport. Then, in 1929, Clarence "Pine Top" Smith released a tune called "Pine Top's Boogie-Woogie." Uncle Benny played blues piano and had a social and working relationship with both Pine Top and Cow-Cow. In fact, Peggie Davenport, a vaudeville entertainer and Cow-Cow's widow, lived with Uncle Benny and his wife as a boarder until her death in the early 1980s. Mykel knew her as Miss Peggie, the nice but mysterious old lady with trunks full of glittery costumes stored in Uncle Benny's basement.

Focus on Language

Answer Key

Column A
1. c, e The coffee was *flavored* with warmth and laughter.
2. b, f We *sipped* our coffee.
3. a, h The singer's voice *rang out* from the radio.
4. d, g The people *gathered* around the president.

Verbs with Positive Connotations	*Verbs with Negative Connotations*
1. flavored, seasoned (pleasant)	peppered (possibly stinging and unpleasant)
2. sipped, sampled (small and neat)	slurped (sloppy and loud)
3. rang out, resonated (pleasant sound)	blared (loud and unpleasant sound)
4. gathered, assembled (orderly)	swarmed (disorderly and possibly dangerous)

Unit 9. "Thomas Iron-Eyes" by Marnie Walsh

Preparing to Read

Additional Background Information
The following information augments the material presented under "Preparing to Read." Students should be encouraged to read this information. Admittedly, the following overview falls far short of providing a complete look at Native Americans. It serves only as a very general introduction to the cultures of a very complex people. To find more resources about Native Americans, the reader should use the bibliography and the "Additional Works of Interest" section.

Native American, with an uppercase *n,* refers to the original inhabitants of North America, sometimes referred to as Indians, whereas native American, with a lowercase *n,* refers to any person born in the United States, regardless of race. The poem "Thomas Iron-Eyes" contains many references to Native American (specifically Plains Indian) culture. Native Americans fall into two broad groups: Eastern and Western. The former are sometimes referred to as woodland Indians because they lived and hunted in the woodlands or great forests of the eastern portion of the United States. The Western Indians in large measure are comprised of tribes known as the Plains Indians, primarily because these tribes lived and hunted on the Great Plains, west of the Mississippi River. The Plains Indians are the Native Americans most often (and usually erroneously) depicted in Hollywood movies about the American Wild West. In particular, films about the U.S. Cavalry show the Plains Indians in an unfavorable light, thus perpetuating the stereotypes.

Native Americans are far from monocultural. Within each of the two general groups there are many different tribes, each one with its own name and unique language and rich culture. Before the arrival of European settlers, Native Americans inhabited almost every area in North America, mainly because they could so ably adapt to their environment.

Many of the original tribes disappeared with the onslaught of European exploration and settlement. For instance, the Mandan tribe of the Missouri River was annihilated by a smallpox epidemic after coming into contact with white traders carrying the deadly disease. Although some tribes didn't disappear altogether, their numbers were greatly reduced as a result of conflict with whites. The Cherokee were forcibly "removed" from eastern United States to reservations west of the Mississippi River. As a result of the many terrible hardships suffered along the way, their journey from east to west became known as the "Trail of Tears."

Although many of the original tribes are gone forever, some tribes survive to this day. The Blackfoot, the Navaho, the Pueblo, and the Cherokee are just a few of the tribes that exist today. Today's Native Americans are moving into the twenty-first century with a renewed commitment to preserving their rich heritage.

The First Reading

The following are only suggestions for working with the poem. The teacher should adapt these suggestions or use other activities appropriate for his or her students.

The teacher could begin by reading the poem out loud in its entirety as students either read along silently or only listen. Or more advanced students could read the poem on their own.

After the initial reading, the students should be asked what they think the poem is about. At this point, it is enough for students to recognize that the poem deals with Native Americans, death, and death rituals. If none or only a few of the students recognize the topic, there is no reason for concern. The poem will become clearer to students with additional readings. During the activity called "Sharing the Possibilities," the class will explore the poem in depth.

A Closer Look

Classroom testing of *Distant Thunder* has shown that the topic of the Native American is of very high interest to ESL students. Because they enjoy researching and presenting material on this topic, this activity is well worth doing.

Sharing the Possibilities

Students should be encouraged to refer to the poem to support their answers as well as their reasons for changing a previous response. Even though students are encouraged to review their responses and change them when necessary, it is important for the teacher to act as a moderator or guide, not as meaning giver or judge. However, the teacher can provide literal rather than interpretive meanings for any words that confuse the students.

After the final stanza has been examined, the poem should be reread from beginning to end. Students should be encouraged to ask each other questions and to compare responses. The teacher should provide answers to questions about vocabulary or culture but resist giving his or her interpretation of the poem.

Extending the Reading Experience

Because this is an imaginary video production, students do not need a video camera or even any experience making videos. In small groups called production teams, students should decide on how best to audiovisually interpret the poem. This activity will take several class periods to complete. However, it is well worth the effort and time for several reasons: (a) it requires a close examination of the poem, (b) it allows for a variety of creative interpretations of the poem, and (c) it requires a lot of negotiation of meaning (i.e., it is highly communicative). The class should be reminded often to use the context of the poem as well as their interpretations as their guides.

Focus on Language

Shifts in Tense

Understanding tense aspect and modals is important to understanding the poem. "Thomas Iron-Eyes" moves from past to present (stanza one) to present counterfactual (stanzas two and three), then back to present again and finally to future (stanza four). Below are the main verbs found in stanza one.

Simple Past		Past Continuous	Simple Present
woke	knocked	was coming	lie
painted	greased		finds
tied	took		
dwelt	was		
crept	put		

Stanza one contains recent past events and present time.

In stanzas two and three, the modal *would* is used repeatedly. *Would* is used implicitly in such lines as "[would (have)] Borne me in honor" and "[would] Lie down to wait my needs." *Would* as it is used in the poem expresses what might have been if circumstances had been different. It is used in the unreal or counterfactual sense. Counterfactual conditionals express impossible events: for example, "If this were another time, another life, another place, I would have an honorable burial." In this sentence, the *if* clause is strongly negated.

The first line "Another time, another life, another place" signals that the actions that follow happened in the distant past and are perhaps no longer possible.

Below are the main verbs used in stanza four.

Simple Present		Future
am	grows	will be put
run	abound	will seal
rust out	slips	will (not) hear
sits	wait	
stink	stand	

Stanza four contains present events and conditions and future time.

Glossary of Terms

character   an imagined person who lives within a story, although characters can also be animals and even objects with human traits. A character who dominates a story is called a major or main character while less important characters are called minor.

characterization   the methods by which an author reveals a character's personality and motives and thus makes a character appear to be real (alive) to the reader. To accomplish this the author may describe a character's physical appearance as well as thoughts and actions.

chronological order   the organization of events according to the order of time.

closed form verse   poetry that follows a pattern of rhyme and rhythm. The Shakespearean sonnet and Japanese haiku are good examples of the closed form with their prescribed number of lines, the former also adhering to a rhyme scheme or pattern.

connotation   the additional meaning a word carries, usually associated with the emotions that the word suggests. Words that have essentially the same dictionary meaning can nevertheless have very different connotations. For example, *eat* has a neutral connotation while *gorge* and *dine* have negative and positive connotations respectively. A word gets its connotation from the contexts in which it is frequently used.

denotation   the dictionary meaning of a word. Often two or more words can have the same denotation but, because of the words' emotional overtones, have very different connotations. (See the term *connotation*.)

figurative language   language that creates a picture in the mind often by comparing seemingly unlike things. This can result in a fresh way of looking at everyday objects and otherwise ordinary events and people.

flashback   a device by which an author reveals events that happened prior to the beginning of a story. The author may use various ways to present a flashback such as dream sequences, reveries, and dialogues.

idiom   an expression whose use and meaning are peculiar to a given language.

imagery   words that evoke the senses—sight, sound, touch, taste and smell. The words are used in such a way as to excite the emotions. Abstractions, such as despair and loneliness, can be understood through a lone image or collection of images, in this case, the buzz of a single housefly.

limerick   an example of the closed form, the limerick's primary subject matter is the manners, morals, and peculiarities of people. They are usually humorous and were probably originally handed down orally.

literal language   language that is concrete and not meant to represent an abstraction. The opposite of figurative language.

metaphor   a comparison or analogy between two seemingly unlike things in which one is given the characteristics of the other. In the metaphor, *Amy plowed through her work,* Amy is being ascribed the characteristics of a plow—something that moves quickly forward oblivious to obstacles that might lie in its path.

narrative   the account of an actual or fictional event told in a story or poem.

narrator   the person who tells the story. (See *point of view.*)

open form verse   poetry that does not follow a set pattern of rhyme or rhythm. The opposite of closed form.

point of view   the perspective from which a narrative is told. It answers the question of who is telling the story. Short stories, novels, and even poems contain points of view. They can be told in the *first person* point of view (using first person pronouns). In this case, the person telling the story is usually a major participant in the narrative and is therefore called the narrator. Examples of first person point of view can be found in "Farewell," "Jobs," "The Circuit," "Saturday Morning Memorial," and "Thomas Iron-Eyes." Narratives can also be told in the *third person* (using third person pronouns). Here, the person telling the story is a non-participant and is usually not called a narrator. Examples can be found in "Doors," "La Puerta," "The Purchase," and "Wilshire Bus."

prose   unlike poetry or verse, written or spoken prose has an irregular rhythmic pattern. It is closer in form to everyday speech.

rhythm   the repetition of specific sounds or the repetition of stressed and unstressed syllables. Rhythm heightens the emotional response of readers.

rhyme   a pattern of words in which vowel sounds are the same. This is known as exact rhyme. Various other forms of rhyme exist, including slant rhyme in which the final consonant sounds of words match while the vowel sounds do not. Like rhythm, rhyme intensifies the reader's experience. (Also spelled rime.)

scenario   an impromptu minidrama, a scenario does not have prepared lines to memorize and rehearse or to read as in a role play. Instead "actors" are simply given a kind of predicament in which humans might find themselves. Anticipating each others' behavior, they devise a plan of action for dealing with the dilemma. The scenario's plot cannot be predicted. In this way, the scenario unfolds much like life does.

setting   the day, year, or century and physical locale in which a story takes place. Other elements that comprise setting are the environmental and social conditions.

simile   like a metaphor, a simile draws an analogy between two dissimilar things in which one is given the characteristics of the other. Unlike metaphor, however, similes use connectives such as *like* and *as.*

stanza   a recurrent grouping of lines in a poem made in terms of patterns of rhyme and rhythm. A stanza resembles a paragraph of prose in that ideas shape both units.

symbol   a concrete object that suggests another level of meaning beyond the object. For example, the dove is a symbol of peace.

Bibliography

Carter, R., and Michael Long. *Teaching Literature.* New York: Longman, 1991.

Collie, J., and S. Slater. *Literature in the Language Classroom: A Resource Book of Ideas and Activities.* Cambridge: Cambridge University Press, 1987.

Curtin, Philip D. *The Atlantic Slave Trade: A Census.* Madison: University of Wisconsin Press, 1969.

DiPietro, Robert J. *Strategic Interaction: Learning Languages through Scenarios.* Cambridge and New York: Oxford University Press, 1987.

Griffin, Rodman D. "Illegal Immigration." *CQ Researcher,* 24 April 1992, 363–68.

Harris, J. William, ed. *Society and Culture in the Slave South.* London: Routledge, 1992.

Low, W. Augustus, and Virgil A. Cliff, eds. *Encyclopedia of Black Americans.* New York: Da Capo Press, 1984.

Min, Pyong Gap. "An Overview of Asian Americans." In *Asian Americans: Contemporary Trends and Issues,* ed. Pyong Gap Min, 16–18. Thousand Oaks, CA: Sage Publications, 1995.

"Nisei." *Britannica Online.* <http://www.eb.com:180/cgi-bin/g?DocF=micro/426/43.html> [Accessed 07 March 1998].

Rosenblatt, Louise M. *Literature as Exploration.* New York: Modern Language Association, 1983.

Smith, Page. *Democracy on Trial: The Japanese-American Evacuation and Relocation in World War II.* New York: Simon and Schuster, 1995.

U.S. Bureau of the Census. *1990 Census of Population, General Population Characteristics, United States Summary* (CP-1–1). Washington, D.C.: U.S. Government Printing Office, 1993.

Webster's New Collegiate Dictionary. Springfield, MA: G. and C. Merriam Co., 1974.

Williams, Michael W., ed. *The African American Encyclopedia.* New York: Marshall Cavendish Corp., 1993.

Zamel, Vivian. "Writing One's Way into Reading." *TESOL Quarterly* 26 (1993): 463–85.

Additional Works of Interest

General

Gioseffi, Daniela, ed. *On Prejudice: A Global Perspective.* New York: Anchor Books, 1993.

Lambert, Wallace E., and Donald M. Taylor. *Coping with Cultural and Racial Diversity in Urban America.* New York: Praeger, 1990.

Thomas, Gail E., ed. *U.S. Race Relations in the 1980s and 1990s: Challenges and Alternatives.* New York: Hemisphere Publishing Corp., 1990.

African-Americans

Resource Books

Campbell, Edward D., Jr., ed. *Before Freedom Came: African American Life in Antebellum South.* N.p.: Museum of the Confederacy and the University Press of Virginia, 1991.

Coughtry, Jay. *The Notorious Triangle: Rhode Island and the African Slave Trade, 1700–1807.* Philadelphia: Temple University Press, 1981.

Dubois, W. E. B. *The Suppression of the African Slave-Trade to the United States of America, 1638–1870.* Baton Rouge: Louisiana State University Press, 1969.

Fogel, Robert William. *Without Consent or Contract: The Rise and Fall of American Slavery.* New York: W. W. Norton, 1989.

Fox-Genovese, Elizabeth. *Within the Plantation Household: Black and White Women of the Old South.* Chapel Hill: University of North Carolina Press, 1988.

Gutman, Herbert G. *The Black Family in Slavery and Freedom, 1750–1925.* New York: Pantheon Books, 1976.

Kolchin, Peter. *Unfree Labor: American Slavery and Russian Serfdom.* Cambridge: Belknap Press of Harvard University Press, 1987.

Ogle, Patrick. *Facets African-American Video Guide.* Chicago: Facets Multimedia and Academy Chicago Publishers, 1994.

Smith, Jessie Carney. *Black Heroes of the 20th Century.* Detroit, MI: Visible Ink Press, 1998.

Thomas, Hugh. *The Slave Trade.* New York: Simon and Schuster, 1997.

Supplementary Readings

Angelou, Maya. *I Know Why the Caged Bird Sings.* New York: Random House, 1996.

Armstrong, William H. *Sounder.* New York: Harper and Row, 1985.

Delany, Sarah Louise, and A. Elizabeth Delany. *Having Our Say: The Delany Sisters' First 100 Years.* New York: Dell, 1994.

Elder III, Lonne. "Sounder." In *Best American Screenplays,* ed. Sam Thomas, 392–424. New York: Crown Publishers, 1986.

Hamilton, Virginia. *The House of Dies Drear.* New York: Macmillan, 1984.

Hamilton, Virginia. *M. C. Higgins, the Great.* New York: Simon and Schuster Children's, 1998.

Hamilton, Virginia. *Zeely.* New York: Simon and Schuster Trade, 1998.

Mazer, Norma Fox. *A Figure of Speech.* New York: Dell Publishing, 1973.

Myles, Mykel D. *Crossroads.* Highland Hills Village, OH: Writing Center, Cuyahoga Community College, 1993.

Myles, Mykel D. *The Eye of the Storm.* Cleveland, OH: Burning Press, 1994.

Myles, Mykel D. *Saturday Morning Memorial.* Cleveland, OH: Crossroads Wizard Publishing, 1994.

To order Mykel Myles' books, contact him via the Internet at MykelD@hotmail.com

Yep, Laurence. *Dragonwings.* New York: Harper Row, 1975.

Sound Recordings

Armstrong, William H. *Sounder.* Performed by Avery Brooks. HarperCollins, 1992. Audiocassette.

Davenport, Charles Cow-Cow. *The Complete Recorded Works.* Document 6040, 1993. Compact disc.

Hamilton, Virginia. *M. C. Higgins, the Great.* Narrated by Roscoe Lee Brown. Unabridged. Recorded Books, 1993. Six audiocassettes.

Hamilton, Virginia. *Zeely.* Read by author. Caedmon TC1443, 1974. Audiocassette.

The Roots of Rap. Various artists including James Pine Top Smith. Yazoo 2018, 1996. Compact disc.

Video Recordings

Amistad. Directed by Steven Spielberg. Produced by Steven Spielberg, Debbie Allen, and Collin Wilson. 155 min. Dreamworks, 1998. Videocassette.

Black Americans of Achievement. Twelve-part series. Produced and directed by Rhonda Fabian and Jerry Baber. (30 min. each) Schlessinger Video Productions, 1992. 12 videocassettes.

Black Americans of Achievement: Video Collections II. Ten-part series. Directed by Amy A. Tiehel. Produced by Jerry Baber and Amy A. Tiehel. (30 min. each) Schlessinger Video Productions, 1994. 10 videocassettes.

A History of Slavery in America. Produced and directed by Rhonda Fabian and Jerry Baber. 30 min. Schlessinger Video Productions, 1994. Videocassette.

The House of Dries Drear. Directed by Allan Goldstein. Produced by Valerie Shepherd and Joseph Dennis. 116 min. Public Media Video, 1984. Videocassette.

I Know Why the Caged Bird Sings. Directed by Fielder Cook. Produced by Jean Moore Edwards. 96 min. MCA Distributing Corp., 1998. Videocassette.

Sounder. The Rainbow Group. 105 min. Paramount Home Video, 1984. Videocassette.

Asian-Americans

Resource Books

Agarwal, P. *Passage from India: Post-1965 Indian Immigrants and Their Children: Conflicts, Concerns, and Solutions.* Palos Verdes, CA: Yuvati, 1991.

Haines, D. W., ed. *Refugees as Immigrants: Cambodians, Laotians, and Vietnamese in America.* Totowa, NJ: Rowman and Littlefield, 1989.

Hongo, Garrett, ed. *Under Western Eyes: Personal Essays From Asian-America.* New York: Anchor Books, 1995.

Niiya, Brian, ed. *Japanese-American History: An A-Z Reference from 1868 to the Present.* New York: Facts on File, 1993.

Portes, Alejandro, and Ruben G. Rumbaut. *Immigrant America: A Portrait.* 2d ed. Berkeley: University of California Press, 1996.

Shankar, Lavina Dhingra, and Rajini Srikanth, eds. *A Part, Yet Apart: South Asians in Asian America.* Philadelphia: Temple University Press, 1998.

Viswanath, R. comp. *Teenage Refugees and Immigrants from India Speak Out.* New York: Rosen Publishing Group, 1997.

Wapner, Kenneth. comp. *Teenage Refugees from Vietnam Speak Out.* New York: Rosen Publishing Group, 1995.

Wong, M. G. "Rise in Hate Crimes against Asians in the United States." Paper presented at the annual meeting of the American Sociological Association, Cincinnati, OH, 1991.

Supplementary Readings

Berh, Edward. *The Story of Miss Saigon.* London: Jonathan Cape, 1992.

Berson, Misha. *Between Worlds: Contemporary Asian-American Plays.* New York: Theatre Communications Group, 1990.

Divakaruni, Chitra Banjerjee. *Arranged Marriage.* New York: Anchor Books, 1995.

Divakaruni, Chitra Banjerjee. *Black Candle: Poems about Women from India, Pakistan, and Bangladesh.* Corvallis, OR: CALYX Books, 1991.

Divakaruni, Chitra Banjerjee. *Leaving Yuba City: New and Selected Poems.* New York: Anchor Books and Doubleday, 1997.

Hagedorn, Jessica, ed. *Charlie Chan is Dead: An Anthology of Contemporary Asian-American Fiction.* New York: Penguin Books, 1993.

Larsen, Wendy Wilder, and Tran Thi Nga. *Shallow Graves: Two Women and Vietnam.* New York: Random House, 1986.

McCunn, Ruthanne Lum. *Thousand Pieces of Gold: A Biographical Novel.* San Francisco: Design Enterprises of San Francisco, 1981.

Mukherjee, Bharati. *The Middleman and Other Stories.* New York: Fawcett Crest, 1989.

O'Connor, Flannery. "The Displaced Person." In *The Collected Stories of Flannery O'Connor.* Flannery O'Connor. New York: Farrar, Straus, and Giroux, 1972.

Rustomji-Kerns, Roshni, ed. *Living in America: Poetry and Fiction by South-Asian American Writers.* Boulder, CO: Westview Press, 1995.

Tan, Amy. *The Joy Luck Club.* New York: Ivy Books, 1996.

Yamamoto, Hisaye. *Seventeen Syllables and Other Stories.* Latham, NY: Kitchen
Table: Women of Color Press, 1988.

Sound Recordings

Boublil, Alain, and Claude-Michel Schonberg. *Cameron Mackintosh Presents Miss
Saigon.* Original London cast recording. Geffen, 1990. Compact discs.
Tan, Amy. *The Joy Luck Club.* Read by author. Abridged. Dove Books on Tape,
1989. Audiocassette.

Video Recordings

Children of the Dust. Produced and Directed by Lisa Seidenberg. 12 min. Carousel
Film and Video, 1991. Videocassette.
Come See the Paradise. Produced by Robert F. Colesberry. Written and Directed by
Alan Parker. 135 min. Fox Video, 1990. Videocassette.
Conquering America. Produced by Public Affairs Television. 30 min. Films for the
Humanities, 1994. Videocassette.
The Displaced Person. Directed by Glenn Jordan. Produced by Matthew N. Herman.
58 min. Monterey Home Video, 1986. Videocassette.
From a Different Shore: The Japanese American Experience. 50 min. Films for the
Humanities, 1996. Videocassette.
Heaven and Earth. Directed by Oliver Stone. Produced by Oliver Stone, Amon
Milchan, Robert Kline, A. Kitman Ho. 142 min. Warner Home Video, 1994.
Videocassette.
The Joy Luck Club. Directed by Wayne Wang. Produced by Wayne Wang, Amy Tan,
Ronald Bass, Patrick Markey. 139 min. DVS Home Video, 1994. Videocassette.
Miss India Georgia. Produced and directed by Daniel Friedman and Sharon Grim-
berg. 56 min. Urban Life Productions, 1997. Videocassette.
Thousand Pieces of Gold. Directed by Nancy Kelly. Produced by Kenji Yamamoto
and Nancy Kelly. 105 min. Hemdale Home Video, 1992. Videocassette.
Without Due Process: Japanese Americans and World War II. By Gerald and Misha
Griffith. 52 min. New Dimension Media, 1992. Videocassette.

Latinos

Resource Books

Atkin, S. Beth. *Voices from the Fields: Children of Migrant Farmworkers Tell Their
Stories.* Boston: Little and Brown, 1992.
Blea, Irene I. *La Chicana and the Intersection of Race, Class, and Gender.* New York:
Praeger, 1992.
Heer, David M. *Undocumented Mexicans in the United States.* Cambridge: Cam-
bridge University Press, 1990.
Hero, Rodney E. *Latinos and the U.S. Political System: Two-Tiered Pluralism.*
Philadelphia: Temple University Press, 1992.

Jiménez, Francisco. *Poverty and Social Justice: Critical Perspectives.* New York: Bilingual Press, 1987.

Kanellos, Nicolas, ed. *The Hispanic-American Almanac: A Reference Work on Hispanics in the United States.* Detroit: Gale Research, 1993.

National Commission on Migrant Education (United States). *Invisible Children: A Portrait of Migrant Education in the United States: A Final Report of the National Commission on Migrant Education.* Washington D.C.: GPO, 1992.

Owens, Louis. *The Grapes of Wrath: Trouble in the Promised Land.* New York: Twayne, 1996.

Stanley, Jerry. *Children of the Dust Bowl: The True Story of the School at Weedpatch Camp.* New York: Crown, 1992.

Williams, Norma. *The Mexican American Family: Tradition and Change.* Dix Hills, NY: General Hall, 1990.

Supplementary Readings

Burciaga, José Antonio. *Spilling the Beans.* Santa Barbara, CA: Joshua Odell Editions, 1995.

Jiménez, Francisco. *The Circuit: Stories from the Life of a Migrant Child.* Albuquerque: University of New Mexico Press, 1997.

Rodriguez, Consuelo. *Cesar Chavez.* New York: Chelsea House, 1991.

Steinbeck, John. *The Grapes of Wrath.* New York: Viking Penguin, 1989.

Steinbeck, John. *The Pearl.* New York: Penguin Books, 1992.

Steinbeck, John. *Of Mice and Men.* New York: Penguin Books, 1993.

Sound Recordings

Cesar Chavez: The California Grape Boycott. Interview. 60 min. Canadian Broadcasting System, 1972. Audiocassette.

Steinbeck, John. *The Grapes of Wrath.* Read by Henry Fonda. 58 min. Harper Audio, 1978. Audiocassette.

Video Recordings

The Ballad of Gregorio Cortez. Directed by Robert M. Young. Produced by Moctesuma Esparza and Michael Hausman. 105 min. Nelson Entertainment, 1988. Videocassette.

Cesar Chavez. Hispanic and Latin American Heritage Video Collection. Produced by Andrew Schlessinger. 30 min. Schlessinger Video Productions, 1995. Videocassette.

In Service to America. Produced and directed by Paige Martinez and Sam Sills. 57 min. PBS Video, 1995. Videocassette.

Steinbeck, John. *Of Mice and Men.* Directed by Gary Sinise. Produced by Russ Smith and Gary Sinise. 110 min. MGM/UA Video, 1992. Videocassette.

Steinbeck, John. *The Grapes of Wrath.* Directed by John Ford. 129 min. CBS/Fox Company, 1988.

Native Americans

Resource Books

Brown, Dee. *Bury My Heart at Wounded Knee: An Indian History of the American West.* New York: Henry Holt and Company, 1995.

Champagne, Duane, ed. *Chronology of Native American History from Pre-Columbian Time to the Present.* Detroit: Gale Research, 1994.

The Indians. Time Life Books. New York: Time, 1973.

Johnson, Michael G., ed. *The Native Tribes of North America: A Concise Encyclopedia.* New York: Macmillan Press, 1992.

Waldman, Carl. *Atlas of the Native American Indian.* New York: Facts on File, 1985.

Yenne, Bill, ed. *The Encyclopedia of Native American Indian Tribes: A Comprehensive Study of Tribes from Abitibi to the Zuni.* N.p.: Arch Cape Press, 1986.

Supplementary Readings

Allen, Paula G., ed. *The Voice of the Turtle: American Indian Literature: 1900–1970.* New York: Ballantine Books, 1995.

Dove, Mourning. *Coyote Stories.* Lincoln, NE: University of Nebraska Press, 1990.

Man-Who-Stands-Looking-Back. *Dee Brown's Bury My Heart at Wounded Knee.* Chicago: Dramatic Publishing, 1973.

Momaday, Scott N. *The Way to Rainy Mountain.* Albuquerque, NM: University of New Mexico Press, 1969.

Peyer, Bernd C., ed. *The Singing Spirit: Early Short Stories by North American Indians.* Tucson: University of Arizona Press, 1991.

Walsh, Marnie. *A Taste of the Knife.* Boise, ID: Ahsahta Press, 1976.

Sound Recordings

Brown, Dee. *Bury My Heart at Wounded Knee.* Discussion by author. The Center for Cassette Studies, 1974. Audiocassette.

Heartbeat: Voices of First Nations Women. Smithsonian/Folkways Recordings, 1995. Compact disc.

Music for Native Americans. Performed by Robbie Robertson and the Red Road Ensemble. Capital Records, 1994. Compact disc.

Social Dance Songs of the Iroquois. The Allegheny River Singers. JVC Classics, 1998.

Spiritual Songs, Traditional Chants: Flute Music of the American Indian. Gold Collection. Retro, 1997. Compact disc.

Videos

The Broken Chain. Directed by Lamont Johnson. Produced by Lamont Johnson and Cleve Landsberg. 93 min. Turner Home Entertainment, 1993. Videocassette.

Lakota Woman: Siege at Wounded Knee. Directed by Frank Pierson. Produced by Fred Berner. 118 min. Turner Home Entertainment, 1994. Videocassette.

The Native Americans. Six-part series. Directed by John Borden. Produced by Michael Grant and Patricia Foulkrod. (50 min. each.) Turner Home Entertainment, 1994. Six videocassettes.

Windwalker. Directed by Keith Merrill. Produced by Thomas E. Ballard and Arthur R. Dubs. 105 min. Video Treasures, 1993. Videocassette.

Teaching Literature

Beach, Richard. *A Teacher's Introduction to Reader Response Theories.* Urbana, IL: National Council of Teachers of English, 1993.

Bleich, David. "The Identification of Pedagogy and Research in the Study of Response Literature." *College English* 42 (1980): 350–66.

Bleich, David. *Reading and Feelings: An Introduction to Subjective Criticism.* Urbana, IL: National Council of Teachers of English, 1975.

Culler, Jonathan. "Literary Competence." In *Reader Response: From Formalism to Post-Structuralism Criticism,* ed. J. Tompkins. Baltimore: Johns Hopkins University Press, 1980.

Gregg, Gail P., and Pamela S. Carroll, eds. *Books and Beyond: Thematic Approaches for Teaching Literature in High School.* Norwood, MA: Christopher-Gordon Publishers, 1998.

A Handbook to Literature. Harmon, William, and C. Hugh Holman, eds. 7th ed. Upper Saddle River, NJ: Prentice-Hall, 1996.

Iser, Wolfgang. "The Reading Process: A Phenomenological Approach." In *Reader Response: From Formalism to Post-Structuralism Criticism,* ed. J. Tompkins. Baltimore: Johns Hopkins University Press, 1980.

Karolides, Nicholas J., ed. *Reader Response in the Classroom: Evoking and Interpreting Meaning in Literature.* New York: Longman, 1992.

Langer, Judith A., ed. *Literature Instruction: A Focus on Student Response.* Urbana, IL: National Council of Teachers of English, 1992.

Maley, Alan, and Alan Duff. *The Inward Ear: Poetry in the Language Classroom.* Cambridge: Cambridge University Press, 1989.

Peck, David R. *American Ethnic Literatures: Native American, African American, Chicano/Latino, and Asian American Writers and Their Backgrounds: An Annotated Bibliography.* Pasadena, CA: Salem Press, 1992.

Warren, Myrna Jean. *The Pearl/Of Mice and Men: Curriculum Guide.* Rocky River, OH: Center for Learning, 1998.